Typeset by Jonathan Downes, Andrea Rider
Cover and Layout by SPiderKaT for CFZ Communications
Using Microsoft Word 2000, Microsoft Publisher 2000, Adobe Photoshop CS.

First published in Great Britain by HoA
This edition by CFZ Press

CFZ Press
Myrtle Cottage
Woolsery
Bideford
North Devon
EX39 5QR

© CFZ MMXV

ISBN: 978-1-909488-29-8

Acknowledgements

My unreserved thanks go to my dear wife, Ann, who once again has helped me to get through the often-fraught process of writing another book, and that includes the onerous task of proof reading the original MS. I would also like to acknowledge the invaluable help and assistance given to me by the internationality respected exorcist Mr Terry Stokes. I am also grateful to Ms Terry Graham currently living in Guadalajara, Mexico, for allowing the factual and unnerving account of her brush with an invading entity to be included in this book. In addition, my sincere appreciation goes to the talented mediums Mr Karl Fallon and Mr Patrick McNamara for their assistance with this case. Finally my special thanks go to Mr Richard T Cole for providing the cover artwork

Contents

Part Two

Part Three

Appendices

Introduction

In the course of researching material for this book I was confronted with a multitude of almost unbelievable and differing nuances of opinion and belief when dealing with the subject of demonic or Satanic possession. These took the form of everything from a simple faith in saints and demons espoused by the early, especially medieval Christians, to supposed vampires and the largely self-appointed slayers who take it upon themselves to rid us of these supernatural hybrids. Since vampirism is also arguably a form of possession by an evil spirit, it dovetails easily with the more conventional model. These beliefs acted as a kind of two-way filter, both feeding and evolving into the infinitely greater sophistication and borderline charlatanry of what passes for Christianity in some supposedly Christian schisms in the modern world and there are more of these than one might think.

As far as those who become possessed and are deemed to be in need of exorcism, go there is no defining personality type, because the individuals who display the traditional signs of apparent demonic possession can be either devoutly religious or have no religious affiliations whatsoever. As with mental illness the person may seem absolutely fine on the outside, but this gives no clue as to what is going on inside. This has been likened to a moving vehicle where externally all appears as it should be, but the observer has no idea who (or what) is driving it; usually until it's too late, which is why mental illness and possession often appear virtually identical in nature.

To be sure, there are still many extremely pious and genuine people out there who successfully challenge perceived evil spirits and by their lights wrestle 'that old serpent' Satan to the ground on an almost daily basis. However, there are also individuals and groups of individuals who, although loudly and vociferously proclaiming their scriptural credentials, have an altogether much darker agenda which, they claim, is also founded on biblical principles. It is among these groups that we will find the most appalling, shameless, devious and dangerous hypocrisy imaginable.

Despite this, like the genuine souls of medieval times, they practise various forms of exorcism and deliverance on the road to their usually expensive version of salvation. They continue to proliferate and grow because their right to do so is enshrined in the American constitution; in God we trust indeed. Although belief in demonic possession (or possession by evil spirits, the two are usually synonymous) exists in almost every faith be it mono or polytheistic, because the remedies are very similar for the sake of clarity and simplicity I have chosen to concentrate on the Christian version. One thing that will become increasingly clear is that there is little or no difference between the phenomena supposedly manifested by these individuals in the name of God and traditional magick and sorcery. It also becomes clear that there exists a primal energy that is neither good nor bad; the end product lies entirely in the hands of the user and this holds true irrespective of the era.

I should emphasise from the outset that I have no intentions of either causing or giving offence, but only to inform and hopefully offer alternative ways of viewing traditional and long held beliefs. Some of these beliefs were adapted from much older traditions into the developing churches and have continued to flourish in that form. However, some religious schisms are trying to present these ancient teachings and techniques as something quite new when they are not, and in the course of this book, we look at how this has been done. I should add that some of the source material the book draws from was written in much simpler times when the 'truth' was very much the work of earnest people with an agenda to pursue, but I have tried to allow for that; hopefully I succeeded. Finally, where appropriate I have used the spelling 'magick' when referring to genuine practitioners and examples of this most rarefied art to differentiate between stage illusions and genuine examples of thaumaturgy.

PART ONE

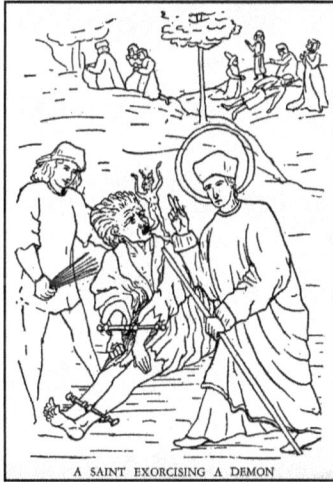

A SAINT EXORCISING A DEMON

Chapter 1
Personal Demons

There are a few categories of paranormal and supernatural phenomena that are almost too terrifying to contemplate. One is poltergeist manifestations, and the other - depending on one's religious outlook - is even worse and that is the possession of a human being by an evil spirit or demon. This second example, again depending on whether one is religious or not, helps focus and define belief, because if there is such a thing as demonic (or evil) possession, then logically to counteract this there should also be a nominal force for good. What this might be depends largely on one's culture and/or spiritual outlook and if nothing else it demonstrates the laws of balance in the cosmos, high and low, salt and sweet, good and evil...and the ultimate Gnostic and much imitated truth: 'As above, so below'.

It also implies that if both ends of this particular spectrum do exist then, traditionally, the 'good' i.e. 'God' should vanquish the bad, i.e. Satan or one of his lieutenants. The whys and wherefores of this, although obviously important, are not the subject of this book, but are based around the supposition that since God made the cosmos (and Satan), then He has the final say over who (or what) is (or is not) allowed. Unfortunately, it does not explain why these situations occur in the first place, but this tends to be attributed to the inherent weakness and fallibility of human beings.

The reason that I do not intend to get mired in the theology of all this is because it is long, complex and may well serve to cloud the issue with individual elements of inflexible dogma and prejudice. Although the subject of possession and its symptoms may not be based entirely on faith alone, it exits in some very deep and murky religious waters. However, theology or not, it does appear that demonic possession, or something very like it, can and does occur. There are several classic literary examples of this and one of the most famous is the notorious incident in medieval France that was dramatised by Aldous Huxley in his 1952 book *The Devils of Loudon*. The book was later filmed by the late *enfant terrible* of British cinema, Ken Russell, in 1972 as *The Devils,* and it is a film that in its unflinching portrayal of the horrendous savagery employed by the church and state still, to this very day, is not easy to watch and has the ability to shock.

Incidentally, apart from some typically florid embellishments (the elaborate set pieces at the Court of King Louis VIII in particular are a revelation); Ken Russell stays pretty much with the facts that led to the accusations of sorcery and heresy levelled at Fr. Urbain Grandier. Although it concentrates on the travails of one man, such excessively cruel treatment was standard fare for those adjudged guilty of the crime of heresy. We shall come across this again in more detail a little later along with the events that, although infinitely less brutal, served as the background to the all time standout genre film *The Exorcist*. However, unlike the events depicted in the back story to *The Exorcist*, at least one other famous exorcism described in this book, excluding the events in Loudon, may have had other, more pragmatic and even political, origins and purposes.

I suppose I should declare an interest here, because unlike most of those who have examined the phenomenon of exorcism and all the occasionally unsavoury odds and ends that attach themselves to it, I have been exorcised. This occurred in 2002 and the ritual (if that's what it could be called) took place, not in the quasi-mystical setting in a church, or even one of the overheated services conducted under the more boisterous aegis of a Pentecostal/evangelical/charismatic meeting, but at around 2:00am in the locker room of my place of work at the time. The 'exorcist', I'll call him 'John', (it's not his real name, but he values his privacy and I respect that) was a South African fellow employee in his mid-thirties who had dabbled extensively in various areas of esoteric interest involving a combination of Sufi mysticism and religion. He was interested in (and practised) yoga and meditation, and was also a qualified fitness instructor; an interesting combination of talents.

We were both on the same shift and had struck up a friendship based around mutual interests including some aspects of Sufi teaching and in addition we had often mulled over theories regarding the survival of consciousness after physical death. There was no real precursor to the 'exorcism'. It was quite spontaneous and developed from one of our discussions during which he stared at me intently and told me that I had a 'spirit' attached to me. 'John' told me that it was a debilitating negative influence and it had been there for several years. Then, right out of the blue, he went on to tell me some personal details about myself and in particular that I had a latent problem with my right knee and that it would become progressively worse: he was absolutely correct. Some of the information related to the here and now and some of it would happen later; it all did. I've thought about this quite often since then, wondering if I was conflating events that happened subsequently make them fit, but that was not the case, the events predicted occurred exactly as he said and in the order he said they would.

While I was still trying to make some sense of what I had just heard, he leaned across the table and, almost in a whisper, asked me if I would like him to remove the spirit. I was initially doubtful because I had never had any inkling that anything like this had occurred, but being aware that this can happen I was curious. I asked if he could really do this and he said yes, he could. He suggested that it should be done quickly and now was as good a time as any. I asked him a little more about this 'spirit'. What was it and how had it become attached to me?

According to 'John' the spirit was male (they have genders apparently, at the time I had assumed that a spirit was non-gender specific, but from experience I now know differently). It was spiteful and bitterly resented the fact that, as human beings we were corporeal and could experience emotions and feelings it could not. It had become attached to me as a direct result of my leisure time pursuits of investigating claims of supernatural occurrences; I could accept that since, over the years, I had been involved in some close encounters with what one might describe as 'spirit entities', and other manifestations of the paranormal.

I asked 'John' what he had in mind, so he suggested that we go to the locker room, which was empty at that time, the staff all being either at work or on meal breaks. I was unsure but still extremely curious and asked if this would take long. John said it should take around 10 to 15 minutes and from what I have since learned that was extremely unusual because they can sometimes last for months of repeated rituals. We both got to our feet and went to the locker room; although I had at least some experience of paranormal phenomena this was the first time that I was the 'main event'. When we entered the locker room we checked to ensure no one else was there and John, with no further ado, began. I asked what I had to do and he told me to remain calm and if possible not to react to what he did, or panic if anything manifested.

I asked if I should close my eyes, but he said it was up to me, just whatever I was most comfortable with; I kept them open! I stood front of him and he stepped back about two or three paces and literally jumped towards me intoning a chant of some kind, his arms were outstretched in front of him with his palms towards me. His eyes were wide and his face was a mask of fierce concentration. He was not speaking in English; it was not any language that I recognised. I have heard people 'speaking in tongues' before and since and it did not sound like that either, in fact in retrospect I'm not sure if it actually was a language at all. He did this for a few minutes, continually stepping back and leaping forward repeating the same (unintelligible) phrase. Then he stopped and peered at a point just over my left shoulder, and his voice, which was like a sharp bark, became lower, almost cajoling and what he said, although still unintelligible, changed too.

From my perspective all I could see were the lines of lockers in front of me and of course 'John'. When he began the ritual the sound quality around me changed and became almost hollow with a slight echo yet somehow dampened, it's difficult to explain and I could feel the temperature of the air become lower. I had experienced something very similar previously elsewhere when an entity materialised during an investigation. I was not in any sense afraid and I was totally focussed on what John was doing. Suddenly he stopped altogether and his gaze shifted to a spot directly above my head, he almost whispered that I should not move and that the spirit was leaving.

He reached out his right hand and placed it on my left shoulder and announced that the spirit had now gone completely. Then the strangest thing happened. I fell to the ground as if I had been pole-axed. My right leg just gave way completely and I experienced a really strange and abrupt numbness in my sciatic nerve. Just before he reached out his hand I had felt an odd tingly sensation above my right shoulder blade, not painful just tingly and that was immediately before I dropped to the floor.

John helped me to my feet and advised me that this was to be expected and not to worry; in fact he was pleased that my reaction was not more pronounced. He suggested that I sit down for a moment on a nearby bench, which I did. He assured me that the spirit was gone and would not return and that he had placed a 'block' to prevent any other spirits from entering. He also explained that pretty much everyone has had an encounter with these entities, sometimes they just leave of their own accord and for their own reasons, or sometimes they stay like a kind of passive observer. This did not appear to be a case of vicarious enjoyment either, neither was it in any sense symbiotic. More like a need to observe how human beings live and interact with one another on various levels.

However sometimes, depending on the person, they do try to take over and occasionally they succeed and that is when they manifest in various symptoms that are usually assumed to be 'emotional problems' and treated with an appropriate drug. When that fails the victim can be incarcerated in a psychiatric hospital; of course the difficulty lies in knowing when the condition is medical or spirit created. Due to the condition being wrongly diagnosed, this is apparently why psychiatric institutions often have a reputation for being haunted. Then again it may be the result of the externalisation of the often chaotic frenzy of impulses and impressions that exist in the brains of the truly mentally ill who live there, acting as a kind of psychic 'lure' that attracts some of the lower entities that surround us

The whole procedure had lasted for just over twenty minutes and from my point of view, in that short space of time something indefinable had indeed occurred; something had changed although it was difficult to decide precisely what. Did something actually leave me or did I imagine the whole episode prompted by my own expectations reinforced by what John said and did? Did I imagine the drop in the ambient temperature and the subtle change in the acoustics, or did it actually occur? What I did not imagine was my right leg giving way and falling to the floor, nor did I imagine the tingly sensation just prior to this occurring. So, imagination helped by arousal and expectation and the fact that it was 2:00am, or something very real but, equally, very strange? With the perfect vision of hindsight I'm pretty sure that something bizarre did indeed occur that early morning.

The thing is that since then, as result of my research into the mysteries and anomalies of the paranormal, I have had to conduct three fairly rough and ready exorcisms myself, in each case it involved having to remove 'entities' from my home and fortunately in each case they went. There was no fuss or elaborate ritual; it was case of me asking them, in no uncertain terms, to leave my house. Ok, the first time I had to do it I thought I would feel a bit foolish talking to an ostensibly empty house, but I did not, it seemed the right thing to do, appropriate even...and it worked.

In retrospect is there anything that I would have done differently? I suppose the strange ritual conducted in the locker room was risky for a number of reasons and not just simply because someone might have walked in. What if the entity had put up a fight; what might the outcome of that have been then because some of these beings are profoundly malicious? Anyway, there was no fight as far as I could tell and no one did walk in, and besides, the ritual appeared to have been effective, so all's well that ends well I suppose.

Chapter 2
The Origins of Exorcism

Although, perhaps due to the publicity it receives, it is sometimes regarded as a comparatively recent phenomenon, exorcism (from the Greek word *'exorkizein'*, which means "to bind by oath") and the expulsion of evil spirits from an afflicted person is an ancient tradition that takes many forms. The invading entity is colloquially either known as a demon, (again originating from the Greek *'daimon'*), a being who interacted between human beings and gods, or an 'evil spirit' of some kind. Lucifer and his cohorts who, after starting a war with the heavenly host, were ejected from heaven and became the 'fallen angels' in the sense that they rejected the wishes of Almighty God. Oddly enough, an identical attribute (i.e. an intermediary between human beings and God), is awarded to angels as well.

Because of this, the fallen angels were awarded suitably evil traits and became associated with all that was debased, corrupt and wrong and from that became the archetypes for every demonic entity since then. Lucifer of course, being the ringleader behind all of this, automatically became elevated to the rank of chief demon, viz Satan (or Ha-Satan, sometimes referred to as 'the adversary'). Equally strangely they were also credited with teaching humanity a variety of basic scientific skills, such as astronomy, metallurgy, chemistry and, bizarrely, the use of cosmetics and how to abort foetuses.

Since they were/are inherently evil and have no physical form, they take great pleasure in insinuating themselves into a (usually) unsuspecting human host and using that host for their own ends. Why take over and abuse such humble and flawed constructs as human beings? Well, since the human race is assumed to be the work of God, something that He was apparently well satisfied with, this was the ideal way for Satan and his armies of demons to get their own back. The only way to rid unfortunate human beings of such a horrific fate is to use the power of God against the invading demons and literally drive them out, and this is the basis of the traditional rite of exorcism.

However, the idea that a human being can be overcome, infected or invaded by another entity is far from new and the rite of exorcism by any other name long predates any form of organised religion. In fact, traces of it can be detected millennia ago in cultures where there was no formal religion whatsoever. From a historical perspective it is known that 2000 years ago the priests who operated the polytheistic faiths of ancient Babylon, (modern Iraq), especially those who worshipped the entity Marduk, carried out exorcisms as required. In their opinion, which, surprisingly, is still a prevalent idea, most illness and particularly mental illness, was directly attributable to an invading spirit. As we will discover later in the book modern Christian schisms that practise other versions of this age-old ritual hold exactly the same opinion, and although there are obvious similarities with the old religions they would be loath to admit it.

One of the methods employed by the Babylonian priests to drive out demons has strong similarities with the practise of what we would call 'poppetry' or sympathetic magick. In this instance, the priests would make a small tablet out of clay or something similar and entice or command the invading demon into that. They would then ritually destroy the tablet and - with it - the demon. This is virtually the same as the 'transference' techniques used in other exorcism rituals and should have similar results. This does tend to polarise opinion here though, because as always much depended on how the person being exorcised accepted the validity of (A) they were actually possessed, (B) they had a strong belief in the ability of whoever was conducting the ritual, and (C) that the ritual was going to be effective.

So if the condition was psychosomatic then the enactment, providing it was sufficiently dramatic and enthusiastically delivered, might well have the desired effect. This does not of course rule out the possibility that these demonic entities do exist and represent a very clear and present danger, and if they do manage to take control of an individual they can also be driven out by the use and application of a suitable set of rules. Because make no mistake about it, irrespective of the era or culture and whatever ritual and ceremony is involved, they have to abide by a specific set of rules designed to induce the entity, whatever it is, to leave.

The attitude to mental illness in the present day Middle East is still very ambivalent and in Saudi Arabia those afflicted with mental illness are normally hidden well away from the public gaze. Unfortunately, because many psychiatric illnesses require the use of medications that appear to infringe Saudi Arabia's stringent religious rules on substances that affect consciousness (such as alcohol) they can be very difficult to obtain. In addition, again in Saudi Arabia, since mental illness carries such social stigma there the public regularly assumes that the 'evil eye' has caused the affliction.

Resonances with this are also found in Malaysia where anyone displaying signs of mental distress are said to suffer from 'sakit jiwa', literally 'soul pain'. It is fascinating to see how in some cultures the soul is still regarded as an integral part of the human body even if it is both intangible and invisible. In Europe right up until the late 17th Century, those who were obviously mentally ill were regularly locked away permanently as 'bewitched'. It is very easy to see how mental instability, especially when expressed in sudden and abrupt outbreaks of violence or uncontrolled swearing, such as in Tourette's Syndrome, could be regarded as demonic, or at least something that did not originate from anything Godly.

Ancient Egypt also regarded illness as possibly deriving from a manifestation of the demonic and had a series of rituals designed to help remove it. They were also surprisingly sophisticated as well, since in addition to possession they also recognised various mental illnesses and that they could be helped, if not cured, by the use of what we would call occupational therapies such as painting and dancing. Other belief systems in the region also promoted the use of trepanning to allow the invading entity to either escape, or be driven out through a small hole drilled into the skull. This at least shows that there was a developing understanding that the human brain was the site of essential mental functions that governed both the person and the body.

Chapter 3
Shamanic Exorcism

We should also recall that, as we have seen, the rite of exorcism was not the sole provenance of those who worshipped any particular god, but was and still is operated in areas where no specific god is recognised, and this applies in particular to shamans. The shaman: the word is assumed to derive from the language of the Arctic Tungus people and can mean variants on *'elevated person'*, *'one who is excited'* or *'wise one'*. The word is also said to have originated from *saman* (xaman), which in turn comes from the verb scha-, *"to know"*.

Unsurprisingly Catholicism, although recognising that people can become demonically possessed, sees it slightly differently and the Catholic Encyclopaedia notes that in Tibet a shaman is a Buddhist who has degenerated into demonology. Whatever the origins, the traditional shaman functioned, and - in some societies - still functions, as a mix of healer, sage and magician. Practitioners of modern versions of this venerable tradition appear to be more interested in it as a 'New Age' oriented lifestyle choice with no real understanding of its fundamental place in society.

Unlike the traditional methods employed in, for example, the Catholic ritual of exorcism where the invading entity is driven out by an accepted form of words, i.e. the *'Rituale Romanum'*, in a shamanic culture a different method is employed. Normally the shaman will enter a trance state, often by ingesting a suitable natural hallucinogen such as peyote or ayhuasca. Other time-honoured techniques, such as repetitive drumming and dancing can also be used, but by their very nature these can take time and the chemical alternative is usually more reliable and obviously quicker. While in an altered state of consciousness the shaman will be aware of the spirit beings that inhabit these realms and can even form a relationship with them so that they recognise one another, and if so inclined can co-operate.

The experienced shaman can actually allow him (or her) self to allow one of these 'spirit beings' to share their body. When this form of symbiosis, (and it is a genuine symbiosis because there are mutually beneficial effects) occurs, the shaman can call on the services and abilities of the guest spirit at will by entering a trance. The soul of the person who is possessed is regarded as having been driven out and replaced by the essence of the invading entity, and it is the role of the shaman/exorcist to locate the missing soul, drive out the demon and allow the soul to re-enter its original body. What this appears to amount to is a kind of 'spirit warfare' referred to elsewhere in this book.

Although the shaman can be comforting and friendly towards the possessed person, which is a necessity in all cases of this type irrespective of whether using a shamanic ritual or otherwise, in common with other forms of exorcism, he/she cannot allow themselves to become emotionally involved in any way. To do this would create a weak point and possible point of entry for the evil sprit and only endanger them, despite having the protection of the 'guest spirit'.

Once again the importance of ritual cannot be over-emphasised in how the shamanic exorcism works and the use of specific words and scents is vital to its success. This technique almost exactly parallels elements all of the exorcisms described in this book; for example smells both fragrant and otherwise created by everything from herbal (usually sage) smudge sticks and perfumes, to burning dried dung (and other noxious substances) can be used. In many ways this mirrors the use of incense in normal, mainly orthodox, church services.

The common use of specific words is also revealing; in the case of Catholic exorcism the correct form of words are those laid out in the centuries old *Rituale Romanum*. They have over the years become 'words of power', in effect they have become a magickal invocation. This can been seen daily during the Roman Catholic Mass in the rite of Transubstantiation just before the sacrament of Holy Communion is offered. The form of words used, *'Hoc est enim corpus meum'* (for this is my body), *'Hic est enim calix sanguinis mei'* (for this is the chalice of my blood) are in Latin and, crucially, were one of the tiny number of items not changed during the lengthy Second Vatican Council (Vatican II) in the 1960s when, amongst other radical changes, the Latin (or Tridentine) mass was largely abandoned and the language of the country in which the mass was being said used instead.

It was a move strongly resented by the more conservative elements within the Catholic Church and indeed the Tridentine Mass was, and still is, said in some traditionalist areas, but officially the Church did not approve and prior to the appointment of Pope Benedict tried to eradicate the practise. However, since Pope Benedict (a noted traditionalist and conservative) came to the throne of St Peter he has suggested that local bishops allow it if there is a sufficient demand. He is also known to privately celebrate the Extraordinary Version of the Roman Rite i.e. the Tridentine version as last used in the 1962, pre-Vatican II, version of the Roman missal. Pope Benedict's fondness for tradition is a part of the mindset that qualified him to be the former director of *'The Congregation for The Doctrine of The Faith'*, in other words the former Holy Inquisition.

That said, it is perhaps essential that rather than pandering to modern concerns of fundamental reform to encourage acceptability and larger congregations, religions in general should retain their core values and traditions. This is particularly true of Islam, which has not been altered in any way to suit modern idioms and appetites. In fact, it is argued that the only way to fully grasp and understand the importance and relevance of Islam is to learn Arabic, because it was in Arabic that the tenets of that faith were first transcribed into the Koran from the words of Mohammed. Of course exorcisms are still regularly carried out in Arabic under the rubrics set out in that particular book.

The reason that the original Latin invocation during the sacrament of Communion was left alone was that it was deemed to have accrued considerable 'spiritual power' over the millennia, mainly because the very act of saying it allowed God Himself to be present on the altar during the Mass. This is something that devout believers in the doctrine of the Roman Catholic Church accept as an absolute truth by an act of faith, and although they do not realise it, it is an act of genuine magick. For this reason the use of traditional terminology and methodology are retained in various religious and quasi-religious ceremonies.

Chapter 4
The Loudon Exorcism

The events described at Loudon in these modern, materialistic and rationalist times are presented, not as demonic possession, but as a secular mixture of religious hysteria, obsession, jealousy and sexual repression combined with a personal vendetta. All of this effectively resulted in the state-sanctioned torture and murder of a wayward priest, Fr. Urbain Grandier. That said, there may have been much more to it than that and the case is also believed to be one of the most prolific examples of demonic possession ever recorded. As we will see, while the whole thing may indeed have been a charade, an elaborate and protracted act of revenge, on the other hand there may equally well have been a genuinely terrifying supernatural element to it. As with many of these events, time dilutes much of the detail concerning what actually occurred and, in addition, modern values are very much at odds with older traditions and beliefs and it is so easy to overlook this.

Fr. Urbain Grandier, who was born in 1590 into a fairly wealthy family with political connections, served as parish priest in the French town of Loudon in the diocese of Poitiers. In addition to his role as a confessor to the local Ursuline Convent, he had the reputation of being something of a rebellious free sprit and chose to largely ignore his vow of celibacy and openly conducted affairs with at least two local women. Because both of the women were linked to the French Royal Court through their fathers, these exploits indirectly led to his downfall. By openly flaunting the rules of celibacy he caused considerable outrage and open hostility (or perhaps jealousy) among the Catholic hierarchy in the diocese, and in 1630 he was arrested on charges of immorality.

It was at this point that his political connections saved him and he was discharged and restored to his position as parish priest once more. Grandier's main adversary, the Bishop of Poitiers, had presided over the proceedings while he stood trial and made no secret of the fact that he wanted him out of his diocese. What happened next is rather less clear-cut and there are two versions of what followed, although either way Grandier was eventually immolated at the stake.

In the first version of events it is speculated that, given the manner in which those suspected of sorcery or witchcraft were treated, the Bishop of Poitiers approached another confessor to the local Ursuline convent, a Father Mignon, and asked him to persuade the Mother Superior *'Jeanne des Anges'* (or 'Sister Jeanne of the Angels') to help him. At the Bishop's prompting, Father Mignon approached the Mother Superior who agreed to say that Fr. Grandier had bewitched her, causing her to take fits and fall to the ground writhing, cursing, using the most appalling profanities and 'speaking in tongues'.

It is not too unusual that, in this case, speaking in tongues (a phenomenon now referred to as 'glossolalia', something we will return to) was used to indicate possession by some malign entity. This shows how times have changed, because in modern times at least, Pentecostalists and other Christian evangelicals still claim this is a sure sign that those so affected have been chosen as a channel for the Holy Spirit. Obviously at the time of the events at Loudon this was not the case, and because the circumstances were different such displays were automatically assumed to be demonic. It should be realised that the existence of demons and other evil spirits, especially during this particularly superstitious era, was accepted totally without question, as was the literal truth and authority of scripture.

It should also be noted that given the considerable influence of the Church, (it was also synonymous with the civil authorities in an unhealthy marriage of church and state) sorcery and witchcraft were accepted absolutely because failure to do so was regarded as a major heresy. After all, the Church believed them to be genuine supernatural phenomena, therefore to deny this was to deny Church dogma, which was the undoing of many suspected heretics and of course those suspected of witchcraft during the later witch-burning craze. It went something like this, as with Fr. Grandier 'the question' was put to the suspected witch/heretic. The question, or at least one of the many 'questions', was: *'Do you believe in witchcraft'*?

The accused, already terrified and perhaps hoping to save themselves from impending suffering, might answer with an emphatic and terrified shriek of *'No'*. Bad choice, because the Church did, so here was an immediate heresy requiring further 'persuasion' to obtain the answer the Church wanted. Although it seems strange, in almost all cases the victim should have said yes and avoided the ensuing session of piously inflicted torture. Coincidentally, in extreme examples of what was judged to be possession during that period, similar brutal methods were also used to elicit a successful 'cleansing'. Supposedly nowadays in cases where demonic possession is suspected, no torture is used except for the application of extremely forceful psychological manipulation to an already suggestible individual. Unfortunately the truth is rather different, and there have been several examples in recent years, especially among those using traditional African rituals, where those thought to be afflicted (including children) have been severely beaten and in a few cases actually killed. This is surely a contemporary example of driving out the devil through the application of severe physical punishment

The other version of the events at Loudon suggests that Sister Jeanne had already heard about the sexual exploits of Grandier and having had some contact with him during pastoral visits to the convent, found him extremely attractive and became obsessed by him. In a direct parallel with the concept of a demonic male 'Incubus', this caused her to dream about Grandier in the guise of a 'bright angel' who came to her in the night and persuaded her to have sex with him. This caused her to cry out in her sleep, which the other nuns could hear. The Mother Superior was horrified that she experienced these overtly sexual dreams and the illicit pleasure she obtained from them and performed drastic penances, including flagellation, to assuage herself from the taint of perceived sin. She then discovered that other nuns in the convent were having similar dreams, so she sent for their confessor, Father Mignon, to exorcise the convent of demons, all of which resonates with modern evangelical and charismatic definitions of possession.

Whatever the cause of the disturbances in the convent, and despite all the political machinations in the background, the unfortunate Grandier was eventually accused of sorcery and arraigned before the local Inquisition and asked to explain himself. This resulted in him being put, not only to 'the question' (as it was euphemistically called), but to 'the extraordinary question'. The difference between these related forms of interrogation was quite simple; if put to 'the question' an admission of guilt by the accused nearly always brought the hideous torture to an end. However, an admission of guilt when being asked 'the extraordinary question' did not stop the agony, which continued until the inquisitor, who was normally a priest or under the direction of a priest, had decided it was over.

In any event Grandier, whose legs had been literally smashed to pieces in 'the Spanish boot' during his torture, at no point implicated anyone else or recanted his original story. All to no avail of course and he was found guilty and when due to be burned at the stake he had to drag himself to the pyre on the shattered remains of his legs. He was not even given the mercy of strangulation before burning either (he had been promised this), but the rope at his neck, probably deliberately, had no slipknot. The choice of 'the boot' or 'Spanish boot' as a method of torture was deliberate since, although the use of torture was justified and even encouraged in cases of detecting heretics, the Church decided that blood should not be drawn. Theoretically the savage and merciless compression of the lower legs in 'the boot' was not supposed to draw blood, but of course it did and copiously too. There are also reports of the marrow seeping from shattered bones. This was a truly brutal, fearful and compassionless era in which to live.

This demonstration of Church sanctioned 're-education' served as a milestone in the campaign of its confrontation with Satan at every, and all, opportunity and despite the fact that modern psychiatrists and psychologists can explain away many of the symptoms displayed by the nuns, there are still some unanswered questions. One of the Church-appointed exorcists who took over from Grandier, a Fr. Surin, took the invading demons into his body during one of the many rituals performed in the convent. At the time Surin is credited as having said, *'I have engaged in combat with four of the most potent and malicious devils in hell'*. Unfortunately, he later died insane and screaming in a Jesuit-run monastery. Another exorcist and accuser of Grandier, Fr. Lactance, was cursed by the agonised priest as the flames licked round him on the pyre and his accuser obligingly died almost precisely when and how the priest had predicted.

Whatever the cause and effect of Grandier's murder, the outbreak of possession in the convent ceased and Satan was apparently sent packing. All of this, as far as the Church was concerned, adequately demonstrated the power of both God and his Church. With hindsight and removed from the rabid superstition of the era, we can make our own judgements. Was the whole thing a trumped-up (and surprisingly costly) affair to rid the church of an inconvenient priest, or was Grandier indeed a closet sorcerer who practised a form of Tantrism and sex magick, and were his promiscuous activities both in the community and the convent a part of that? The truth, as always, was written by the victors who had their own powerful agenda so we will never really know. However, there are elements of the case that resonate powerfully with another set of events the occurred, again in France, a few decades earlier.

Chapter 5
The Miracle of Luon

Once again we encounter another apparent possession in medieval France, but this time of a sixteen year old girl, Nicole Obry (sometimes spelled Aubrey) who, according to the legends that surround the case, became possessed by one of the Lords of Hell, none other than Beelzebub Himself. This possession is thought to have taken place in late 1565 when the girl prayed at the grave of her grandfather and according to the existing accounts, she heard her grandfather speaking to her. The voice asked for a pilgrimage to be done on his behalf to help gain his release from Purgatory.

It transpired that this pilgrimage did not take place, which is when the possession began. Perhaps through the alleged contact with her grandfather's spirit, a 'gateway' for the invading entity had been created? Once again this is a theme frequently encountered when dealing with the subject of paranormal and supernatural phenomena, especially regarding the practise of sorcery. 'Purgatory' is, as the name suggests, a place where souls in a state of grace go to be cleansed or 'purged' of impurity prior to entering heaven, and as we shall see the concept finds direct parallels in all of the main monotheistic religions.

At this point the girl began exhibiting many classic signs of possession: screaming, cursing, performing wild physical contortions, becoming swollen and speaking in a strange voice; she also refused to eat and became ill. In a later chapter, we will encounter a nun who exhibited almost identical phenomena, but this was attributed to the power of God not Satan and clearly shows that the diagnosis all very much depended on the person and the circumstances. Fearing the worst, her parents took her to the local church where demonic possession was quickly diagnosed.

The family engaged the services of a Dominican monk, Pierre de la Motte, who apparently succeeded in exorcising several demons that, according to the records, promptly (if surprisingly) departed for Geneva. The main possessor, who identified itself as 'Beelzebub, the prince of the Huguenots' remained; it is also interesting to learn that Geneva was a hotspot of Huguenot, i.e. Protestant, influence. This demon flatly refused to leave unless the Bishop was sent for and personally conducted the exorcism.

The bishop was indeed sent for and duly arrived, and after an initial attempt at exorcism in the church, had Nicole transferred to the cathedral where, after saying a Mass, he began the lengthy task of exorcism. The fact that the original monk they consulted was Dominican is perhaps illuminating since the Dominican order was specifically set up in the 13th Century by Dominic de Guzman (St Dominic) with the purpose of suppressing the perceived Gnostic threat of the Cathars and other Gnostic threats to the church. In fact, one of the basic tenets of the Dominican order was *'To find truth no matter where it might be'*, and they did, with a will. No surprise, then, to discover that it was this very order that was chiefly responsible for running the various Holy Inquisitions that were instigated in Europe. It seems incredible that such enormities of suffering were instigated by this order of monks, because if the records are to be believed, St Dominic was an extremely selfless and genuinely saintly man. However, it is often the case that individuals like these have their pious zeal subverted by others for much darker purposes.

It is worth stopping to consider that along with many of the 'old gods' attached to the beliefs that had preceded Christianity, entities such as Baal, who in Christian demonology is one of the Seven Princes of Hell (the name Baal means 'master' or 'lord') were co-opted to serve as the bogeymen against whom God battled for the combined soul of humanity. I suppose one could, using the modern analogy adopted during the occupation of a territory by the victors following a battle, regard this as a kind of 'hearts and minds' operation. In that respect, the exorcism and expulsion of such a powerful entity was quite a feather in the cap of whoever could achieve it.

To this end the exorcism, like the one years later at Loudon, attracted thousands of thrill seekers and a scaffolding and stage were constructed in order to allow a better view of the proceedings. From the existing accounts, what occurred was suitably dramatic, colourful, occasionally extreme and lasted for around two months all told. The girl displayed feats of great strength and her face became inflated like a bladder; her tongue also protruded grotesquely from her mouth. She also displayed wild contortions where, like other events that occurred much later in the 18th Century at St Medard in Paris (which we will examine in another chapter) she bent herself double backwards so that her heels touched the back of her head. In addition, various conversations between 'Beelzebub' and the bishop took place with the demon asserting that he was there to convince the faithful of the attractions of rejecting the Catholic faith to become Huguenots.

The end came after Bishop de Bours started feeding the girl with communion wafers and consecrated wine, which produced a spontaneous levitation where Nicole was raised some distance (six feet according to the records) above the trestle on which she lay. Seeing this, the assembled faithful redoubled their prayers to God to assist the bishop in his endeavours. Further proof of the possession was shown by allowing selected members of the crowd to touch the girl and even stick pins in her feet to show that she felt no pain. A variant on this was seen during the craze for witch persecutions when 'devils marks' were discovered by pricking the poor wretches with bodkins until a numb spot, impervious to pain, was discovered. In nearly all cases the bodkin was rigged so that the needle retracted into the handle to fake the effect.

The levitation that eventually occurred marked the gradual banishment of the invading demon, until at 3:00pm on the 8th of February, and accompanied by much howling and shrieking, Beelzebub finally left the body of the possessed girl. This was witnessed by the assembled throng who gave thanks to the Bishop and to God for this graphic display of spiritual strength. Nicole was reunited with her family and husband (she was married) and there the matter should have rested, but it did not. As an addendum to this, there are reports that some years later Nicole again displayed signs of what might (or might not) have been another possession when she went temporarily blind and experienced fits. This time there was no fuss about it and the symptoms gradually vanished on their own, which suggest that this may have been hysterically induced. The date of the original successful exorcism was celebrated annually, but ended (along with other reminders of the 'old days') after the French Revolution.

Chapter 6
The Bizarre Cases of Mariam Mankidiyan and Marie-Julie Jahenny

Mariam Mankidiyan

Another example of possession associated with the Catholic Church concerns the various phenomena associated with a woman called Thresia Chiramel Mankidiyan from the Kerela district of India and as with others of a similar calling, the origins of what occurred can be traced back to her early childhood. A precursor to the better-known nun Mother Theresa, she was born in 1876 to formerly well-to-do parents, but gradually through a set of unfortunate circumstances the family were reduced to poverty.

The 'unfortunate circumstances' were brought about by grandfather marrying off seven daughters and selling the family's lands and possessions to fund the obligatory dowry that went with the daughters in any family at the time. Because most of the information about this woman comes from the hagiographies that have been written about her, it is difficult to obtain an objective viewpoint. However from an early childhood, while only perhaps six or seven years old she displayed a clear passion for her faith, something that was actively encouraged by her mother. This is a common trait among those who have displayed, not only signs of possession, but also those who are supposedly stigmatic and prone to displays of religious ecstasy such as St. Teresa of Avila (another saint who could levitate).

Her religious observance involved prolonged periods of intense prayer and fasting, so much so that she lost a considerable amount of weight and her mother tried to dissuade her from going to these extremes. She rejected this eminently sensible advice saying that she wanted to suffer as Christ had done, and this is always a worrying symptom of what amounts to an unhealthy obsession. This is exactly how many of the saints used to behave and was always a precursor to whatever display of what can only be described as 'magick' they manifested. This includes the 'odour of sanctity', bodily luminescence, levitation, bi-location and a host of other bizarre phenomena.

Strangely enough many of these phenomena are also attributed to the corpses of saints including the circumstances whereby some of them did not degenerate in the normal process of decomposition. Because they were demonstrably 'pious' individuals all of this was normally attributed to the power of God manifesting through them, and so it was with Therisa. She is alleged to have displayed all of these phenomena including those of prophecy and the stigmata, although she concealed the marks of stigmata beneath her robes.

It is perhaps telling that although born Therisa, she adopted the name 'Mariam' (Mary) after supposedly being told to do so by the Virgin Mary who she often saw while in ecstatic states. It is reported that she also had visions of the Holy Family who gave her advice as to how to go about her work. It has been speculated that these visions, which are also frequently experienced by shamans and not just those that are claimed for Mariam, are the product of the severe punishment doled out by the obsessively religious to their bodies. It is possible that the human brain is producing hallucinogenic neurotransmitters in an effort to reduce the pain by substituting feelings of peace and contentment, and it might also be that those who desire it actively continue doing this for exactly that purpose. That said it has also been argued that neurotransmitters allow human consciousness to communicate with other entities in other realities

Eventually she began to display signs of what was judged to be demonic possession, the hagiographies describe this as the Lord 'allowing her to be afflicted by demons'. During these 'attacks' she displayed many of the, by now, standard symptoms of possession: paralysis, shrieking and thrashing around, although why this was not seen (and treated) as another facet of her obsessive and hysterical behaviour is unclear. Between 1902 and 1905 she was repeatedly exorcised by her spiritual director, Father Joseph Vithayathil, whose advice she accepted without question. Fr. Vithayathil pondered that she was perhaps being used as a plaything by evil forces.

This mindset is in itself concerning, because even with the best intentions it would only serve to reinforce the prevailing belief that all the symptoms she displayed could have no other causes other than spiritual, irrespective of whether they were 'good' or 'bad'. The exorcisms did tend to introduce feelings of uncertainty and unease in those who had dealings with her on the basis that anyone who was possessed had to automatically be a sinner also. Mariam Thresia, who was eventually beatified in 2000 by Pope John Paul II, did eventually go on to found an order known as the 'Congregation of the Holy Family' and by the time she died in 1926, the order had created a number of schools, convents and an orphanage.

While the alleged phenomena cannot be independently verified and could have been the result of many factors other than the purely spiritual, the evidence of what she achieved is still there to this day. Unfortunately, that is what passes for hard evidence about this pious lady and since the hagiographies, it and some of the other accounts are taken from, tend to be extremely uncritical propaganda exercises, what we have is highly polarised and therefore best viewed with an open mind.

Marie-Julie Jahenny

The Church-related example referred to in the previous chapter shows even more clearly that the dividing line between what is regarded as demonic possession and that which is presumed to be divinely inspired may well be extremely narrow and subjective. This also manifests in the late 19th Century with the case of the French stigmatic and prophet Marie-Julie Jahenny. Although not a nun, she was a member of the still existing 'Third Order of St Francis' which is open to members of the public with a desire to work within the Church; in some ways it resembles the better known *Opus Dei*.

One of her more alarming prophecies concerns an alleged conversation listened to between Christ and Satan: *"I will attack the Church. I will overthrow the Cross, I will decimate the people, I will deposit a great weakness of Faith in hearts. There will also be a great denial of religion. For a time I will master of all things, everything will be under my control even your temple and all Your people."* In fact many of her, as yet unfulfilled, prophesies appear to refer to the 'End Times' and the enigmatic 'Third Secret of Fatima', but one that did seem to hit the mark was the warning about those who conspired to create the 'new mass'; might this refer to the Vatican II Council? In truth several of her prophesies appear to tie in nicely to what has since come from sources that should be opposed to anything remotely relating to the Catholic Church, i.e. the overwrought and doom-laden pronouncements of the End Times evangelists. This of course does not make them in any sense valid, but it does help create and fuel a fertile environment for the activities of various conspiracy theorists of all hues.

However, prophecies aside, Marie-Julie was in the habit of going into ecstasies/trances on a regular basis, sometimes three times per week, and during one of these trances she warned that as punishment for the sins of humanity committed the previous month, the following Monday she would be 'compressed', her limbs would be compressed and her tongue would swell up enormously. A Dr Imbert, who supposedly witnessed what occurred, recorded that with the onset of the ecstasy her head appeared to sink into her body and her shoulders protruded well above her head. Her body both compressed and inflated until it resembled a ball and her tongue swelled to an alarming size forcing her mouth wide open.

Then, apparently, her shoulder blades rotated until they were vertical, and the left side of her body dilated. The doctor, who was in constant attendance, said that he put his hand on her side and there was almost nothing there, but after a few minutes everything returned to normal size and appearance. If true, this is a genuinely disturbing - if dramatic - display of either self-induced mind over matter or something else entirely. The truly amazing thing is that, according to the statements released, apparently God put her through all this physical torture simply to punish her for the sins of mankind.

Again faint chimes of warning start to sound about the nature and reasons for this occurrence because this begins to sound like some kind of justification to explain these unusual phenomena. Just over a century or so earlier, in any other setting, or in any other context, this lady would have been condemned as demon possessed and/or a witch. Incidentally, the attending doctor could find no rational physical explanation to account for what he had seen. In more recent times however, it is recognised that in cases of extreme religious fervour and hysteria, human beings can - and do - make their bodies perform some incredible feats and contortions.

Chapter 7
'The Convulsionists of Saint Medard'

W hile the title, 'convulsionist', may seem self-explanatory, there is considerably more to what occurred here than first meets the eye, although taken in its own right what occurred at St Medard closely matches some of the phenomena exhibited by the Ursuline nuns of Loudon and Nicole Obery at Luon. The events described also appear to reflect what happened to the woman mentioned in the previous chapter. However, the sheer scale of what occurred in 1731 at the Church of St Medard in Paris really upped the ante for suspected possessions, and - in this case - supposed miracles. What happened here were exhibitions of truly alarming and much more extreme phenomena. The focus of these events was attributed to the sanctity of the then deacon of Paris, the appropriately named Francois de Paris, who was a prominent member of the ascetic Jansenist movement.

This Roman Catholic religious schism was noted for its promulgation of the argument that humanity could not attain salvation by its own efforts, but only through a deliberate act of God, a view that was rejected by the Church. The asceticism of the Reverend de Paris took various forms including sleeping on a hard wooden board covered only with a coarse blanket studded with iron wire, and he wore a hair shirt with a spiked belt, and wore no shoes. He refused any form of heating even in mid-winter, and also lashed himself with a metal studded lash. Some of these practises are still allegedly used by the previously mentioned organisation 'Opus Dei'. It is also relevant that the lay followers of the Jansenist movement also had scant regard for their bodily well-being, a trait they shared with groups such as the Cathar 'perfecti', the Bogomils and others.

Although the accounts of the 'miracles' or 'convulsions' seem like the product of a rather inventive, although sick, imagination, they do appear to have some degree of authenticity. While there were several reliable witnesses to the events, the main source for the contemporary accounts came from Louis de Page, a lawyer, and a magistrate, Judge Louis Montegron. It is interesting that the judge initially refused to believe the testimony of his colleague de Page, but - intrigued - he actually went to the church cemetery to witness the events for himself. and the main body of abundant corroboration comes from his written accounts.

The 'miracles' and 'convulsions' began almost immediately after the 1727 internment of Francois de Paris in the church of Saint Medard. When the deacon was placed in his tomb, which was located behind the altar in the adjoining church, a crippled child who had been brought along by his father fell to the floor in an apparent convulsion and was taken outside into the churchyard. Louis de Page who had been in the church witnessed the child, whose leg had been crippled from birth, leap to his feet and caper around while the muscle tissue appeared to reform as he watched. As we shall see, in a slightly different context this apparently spontaneous manipulation of human tissue is a feature found in other cases involving ecstatic trances, and of course possession.

Almost within a matter of hours the local people, the vast majority both ill and of humble means, flocked to the churchyard and a few days later hunchbacks, cripples, lepers and others with similar afflictions arrived seeking a cure. By this time de Page had informed Judge Montegron and he was on hand to witness and record a large number of these apparent 'cures'. One account dated the September 7th 1731 records that many of those present (oddly enough mainly women) were on the ground with their bodies twisted in remarkable contortions. Many were so bent that the back of their heads touched their heels; but all of them were frothing at the mouth and speaking in tongues. In fact special clothing was created especially for the use of the female convulsionists, it was designed so that it was fastened at the ankles to prevent their dresses ending up over their heads, something that the male spectators, and there were many, gawped at.

The men who were present also seemed affected by the general frenzy and started to beat the women with iron bars and heavy pieces of wood. One woman was naked to the waist and one of the men had her flesh grasped with pincers and was twisting it violently; none of this seemed to produce any pain and the men were exhorted to try harder. On yet another day Montegron records that another woman threw herself to the ground and some men, who appeared to be prepared for what followed, pressed six sharp metal poles against her chest leaning heavily on them, the poles did not penetrate her skin and there was no sign of pain; quite the opposite in fact.

Perhaps the most (depending on how one looks at it) grotesque event recorded by the judge involved a young woman seated at a trestle table in the cemetery eating faeces with obvious relish. Montegron continued to record similar events over a period of some weeks, although the vast majority of the phenomena involved the convulsions. Eventually the church authorities put an end to the continuing spectacle, which was drawing huge crowds on a daily basis, by the expedient of simply shutting the church and posting guards outside it. Slowly those displaying the convulsions and other kinds of 'possession' became fewer and fewer, and eventually the phenomenon stopped completely.

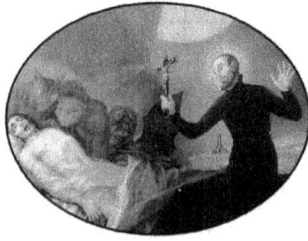

Chapter 8
Exorcism in Early Modern England

Medieval Europe did not exhibit the only cases of possession and exorcism; there are several instances on record in Britain where individuals were considered to be possessed by demons and one of these is the case of Sara Williams (1570-). What makes this more interesting was that Sara (who lived in the village of Denham) was not a Roman Catholic although her employer, Sir George Peckham, was. In fact, Sir George was a 'secret Catholic' since at that time to profess membership of the Catholic faith was to face the possibility of retribution and even execution by the state.

Sir George had in his employ a priest, Robert Dibdale, who decided that Sara was possessed and had to be exorcised forthwith. Sara was in no position to argue about it so she was subjected to a lengthy period of physical and psychological abuse that took the form of being punched, and made to drink a variety of foul (holy) potions. In addition, she was forced to inhale various noxious fumes including burning sulphur. As with the other examples mentioned so far, this was supposedly to force the invading demon to vacate her body. However none of this seemed to work and she remained possessed. As we have seen, the use of violence was a common feature of exorcisms carried out during this period.

Sara was not the only person in Denham deemed possessed. Another teenager, Richard Mainey, was also a suspect. In fact, the village attained such a bad reputation that following the failure of Sir George's priest to elicit results, a small number of Jesuits were sent for. It has to be said that given the anti-Catholic sentiments in Britain at that time these Jesuits must have been rather courageous people. At any rate the Jesuits duly arrived and in the course of the exorcisms that ensued, a number of demons were successfully driven out. There seem to have been five in number; the main demon possessing Sara was 'Mahu'.

The exorcist asked 'Mahu' if there were any more demons with him and he replied that 'all the devils of hell' were there too. This demon was one of many first identified some years later in 1603 by Samuel Harsnett in his vehemently anti-Catholic book,

A Declaration of Egregious Popish Impostures. The other demons discovered were 'Modo', 'Pippin', 'Philpot' and 'Soforce' and also originate in this work, and were designated as *'capitaines'* or 'Princes of Hell'. The Jesuits also found out that many people in the village were possessed for varying times and to various degrees, but on an individual basis, however, they were all possessing Sara simultaneously.

In the case of Richard Mainey, the main possessing demon was Modo, and during the course of his exorcism he was sent to be examined by doctors who could find no convenient medical explanation to account for his symptoms. The relatives of those afflicted, rather than immediately assume that they must be possessed, and make no mistake about it remember that belief in demonic possession was as instinctive as belief in God, often sought medical advice. It is important to appreciate that anything that fell outside the prevailing knowledge of traditional medicine, especially anything that might have neurological origins, was, as a matter of course, frequently ascribed to demonic or Satanic influence. This is why many mentally ill people ended up incarcerated and forgotten about in dank cells, or if sufficient money was available for their care, monasteries and convents. As we have repeatedly seen, to be mentally ill was a sure sign of demonic possession and that is something still found today in some cultures, and also in groups who practise 'deliverance ministry'.

A few years late circa 1620, possession was deemed a suitable condition to be used for financial gain. A woman called Elizabeth Saunders taught Katherine Malpas how to simulate possession in the hope of being given some money through public sympathy. Other instances of exploiting supposed possession for gain were seen when people were seen vomiting up pins and other small objects (evidently a sure sign of possession) falling to the floor, and apparently fitting and exhibiting other signs of traditional possession. Further examination quickly showed that the people involved were confidence tricksters, and they were jailed for their efforts.

Chapter 9
An Irish Exorcism

Bridget Cleary

One relatively recent example of a suspected case of possession stems from late 19th Century Ireland when an unfortunate woman was suspected of being a 'changeling'. This was Bridget Cleary from the village of Clonmel, who was burned to death while having her suspected invading entity removed. In this case, as the name 'changeling' suggests, the possession was not by demons, but by fairies or at least one of the ethereal beings associated with that tradition. According to folklore, a changeling was the offspring of fairies (and occasionally trolls and elves) and was substituted by these mythical creatures for a human child. The reasons for the exchange could vary, but sometimes it was because human children had qualities of love and affection not found in the progeny of fairies.

Other reasons were more pragmatic and the child might be raised as a servant or, showing a considerable degree of pragmatism, to help prevent inbreeding, which - in close communities with a limited gene pool - is always a strong possibility. Of course some of the exchanges were attributed to sheer malice, but this reason was seldom mentioned for fear of upsetting the notoriously touchy inhabitants of the invisible realms. The most dangerous members of the fairy orders were 'the faerie' who, if not openly hostile, were at best utterly indifferent to human beings and for this reason humans referred to fairies in general using non-offensive terms such as 'the good people', and similar anodyne pleasantries. Charms were sometimes placed beside the cot where an infant slept, a set of iron scissors being one of the favourites. Again this introduces resonances with other strands of supernatural lore; one of the most obvious is why iron? Why not something made of glass, wood or bone?

One of the answers to this might lie in the nature of the phenomenon itself, because the use of iron as a tool to ward off a variety of supernatural creatures is commonplace, and may be because iron is a good conductor of electricity. Further hints about this are found in the legends surrounding the Jinni of Middle Eastern legend that can be removed or banished by having an iron chain thrown at them. Is this because the iron interferes with whatever processes animate them while manifesting in our reality and might the presence of an iron artefact in close proximity to a baby's cot similarly help prevent fairies, or their fellow beings manifesting here? If they can manipulate the electromagnetic spectrum at will to 'cross over' (and by our understanding of physics they would have to) then iron could well have a damping effect, or even act as a short circuit.

Is this sheer speculation? Yes, of course it is, but given the nature of the phenomenon it seems to hold at least a shred of credibility. Should the worst occur and the exchange be made, the signs to spot a changeling were continuing ill-health, deformity, Down's Syndrome, severe autism, Spina Bifida and the old favourite, mental illness. Incidentally, it is known that although not restricted to males, in fact male babies have a greater chance of having these defects, so the legend reflected this by noting that male children were more likely to be changelings. The thing here was that Bridget was not identified as a changeling at birth, this occurred a few years after her marriage when the fact that she had not conceived was regarded with some suspicion. Given that this was an unsophisticated, rural and devoutly Catholic area where superstition was rife, and relevant medical issues aside, any suggestion of supernatural interference would find fertile soil in which to flourish.

After a short spell of ill-health, the exact symptoms of which are unknown, the local doctor was summoned to the family home on the 13th of March 1895 and he thought her condition severe enough to require a visit from a priest, who administered the last rites of the Catholic Church to her. Over the next few days a number of friends visited and a few home remedies were suggested. None of these helped, so her husband Michael and her father Patrick accused her of being a fairy and used a traditional method thought to drive out the offending entity.

This involved throwing urine over her (an echo of the tradition of using foul substances to drive out demons perhaps?) and dragging her to the open fire where she was held close to it in the belief that the fairy would take fright and fly off up the chimney. Shortly after this, she disappeared and by the 16th of March rumours were heard saying that she was missing and her husband had stated publicly that the fairies had taken her. By this time the local police had taken notice of what was happening and a search was mounted for her, and on the 22nd of March her badly burned body was eventually found in the scant covering of a shallow grave. The coroner returned a verdict of death by burning.

Her husband and nine associates were arrested for murder and the case began in the April of 1895. It emerged that in the course of the home remedies being tried, the priest, a Father Ryan, had been called to the house and had given Bridget Holy Communion. After the priest left, her husband tried to force-feed her with little success, he then dragged her from the bed to the fireplace and brandished a blazing log in her face. At this point her nightdress caught fire and her husband threw paraffin on her.

Others who were present tried to help, but her husband would not allow it, insisting that she was a changeling and this was the only way to bring the original Bridget back again. The jury was less than impressed by this and Michael was jailed for 15 years, not for murder, but for manslaughter and was released in April 1910 when he left for Liverpool, but eventually ended up in Canada. The whole sad, sorry episode is remembered as the last witch burning in Ireland. Oddly enough the isolated farm cottage where it all occurred was noted as having been built on a 'fairy fort', something else that would not have been lost on the superstitious locals.

Chapter 10
Other Examples of Exorcism

Clara Germana Celle

One case of possession and an attendant demonstration of levitation from the early 20th Century concerned a 16-year-old girl named Clara Germana Celle, who attended a mission school approximately 50 miles from Durban in South Africa. At the beginning of August 1906 she allegedly confessed to the mission priest, Father Horner, that she had entered into a pact with Satan. Following this, on August the 20th, and much to the consternation of the sisters in charge, she began to behave in an extremely alarming manner. She tore and clawed her clothes, broke one of her bedposts, began growling like an animal and started to talk to invisible entities. Each of these symptoms are part and parcel of the classic symptoms of possession.

Clara's condition worsened and she displayed several additional signs of demonic possession, including extreme reactions to contact with holy water; she claimed that it burned her. However, when sprinkled with ordinary water, in spite of being told that it had been blessed and perhaps showing another spin on 'discernment', i.e. she could tell whether or not there was some genuine spiritual involvement, she showed no signs of distress.

The strange reaction to holy water, not uncommon in cases like this, may fall within the speculative realms of quantum physics since the atomic structure of water can allegedly be changed by prayer, and it may be that if Clara was interacting with any entity that was manifesting through her, then the water that had been altered by prayer may well have induced an adverse affect. Might this have a faint resonance with the hypothesis that if, as we saw in the previous chapter, these entities exist at some level within the electromagnetic spectrum that encompasses our understanding of reality, then they might be influenced through manipulation at the subatomic level? A supposition too far? Perhaps, but perhaps not, since there are no known or measurable parameters governing how the phenomenon functions.

The reports state that she refused to have a crucifix, either physically or as a picture, in her presence and she could also evidently sense whether or not concealed religious items were in her vicinity. Fr. Horner also reported various instances of levitation, during which she floated several feet above her bed. He also records that during these episodes she was quite rigid and her clothing did not fall away from her body, but if holy water was sprinkled on her she would descend to the bed and her clothing became loose and normal. Fr. Horner goes on to say that people also tried to physically pull her back down, but were unable to do so.

Other accounts indicate that occasionally she appeared to morph into a reptilian creature. Her entire body became sinuous and she writhed around on the floor while her neck seemed to elongate, further enhancing the snakelike impression. Again we see a possible demonstration that some non-human entity was attempting to change its host into something more acceptable to itself. She reportedly bit one of the nuns on the arm who tried to restrain her, and the mark showed her teeth marks and two small puncture wounds typical of snakebite.

Eventually, in September 1906, permission to carry out an exorcism was granted and Fr. Erasmus performed the ritual assisted by another priest. During this ritual, which was conducted in the presence of many witnesses, the possessing entity stated that it would signal its departure by causing Germana to levitate, which she duly did. However, the entity soon returned and a new, two-day long exorcism was carried out, fortunately this time it was successful and when the entity finally left, it did so accompanied by an incredibly vile stench.

This being the case, it is obvious that certain physical effects of demonic possession, including the presence of a foul smell, share many of the properties normally associated with the methods used to actually expel demons and both are strikingly similar to the symptoms of religious ecstasy. Is it possible that one of the qualifying factors concerns interpretation and context? In other words, could confusion arise due to the similarity between the symptoms, and given a different set of circumstances might Germanas' condition have been viewed in a different manner, i.e. originating from another source?

Hindu and Buddhist mystics have also reported other non-Christian examples of spontaneous levitation, so the phenomenon is not the exclusive right of Christianity, nor as it happens to Islam or Judaism which both have accounts of levitation. The great 13th Century Tibetan yogi, Milarepa, was claimed to possess occult powers including levitation. It was said he could rest, walk and sleep while demonstrating this strange attribute. These abilities have also been attributed to Brahmins and fakirs and interestingly the Japanese assassination cult of Ninja, although this may have something to do with one interpretation of the word, 'Ninja', which can mean 'the art of not being seen'. The Ninja were also associated with being able to 'float' as part of their remarkable martial technique.

While discussing this fascinating subject, in the interests of balance we should consider other purely secular aspects of levitation. Stories of people and entities who are apparently able to defy gravity and hang weightless, suspended in mid-air and to all intents and purposes 'fly', have been with us from the beginning of recorded history. Tales, legends and urban myths old and new provide a source of supposed 'evidence' falling under various headings ranging from dreams and drug fuelled fantasies to stage magic and just perhaps, the genuine ability to levitate. If this is the case, are some long suppressed or forgotten skills surfacing to be used quite unconsciously. Skills that we may have inherited from other sources and remembered only at a cellular level.

The desire to fly, to posses the ability to soar free above the ground has been a common aspiration among human beings since time began. We have long forgotten how to achieve this at will, but the desire and genetic memory still remain. In pursuit of our desire for flight, we have, through developments in technology, designed, and built various mechanical devices that will - in fact - carry us through the air. This however does not satisfy the atavistic desire for the free, unfettered flight we occasionally experience while dreaming. Leaving aside for the moment the religious and chemically induced tales, factual accounts of independently witnessed demonstrations of physical levitation are notably rather thin on the ground, but perhaps the best of these concerns the almost legendary 19th Century physical medium, Scottish born Daniel Dunglas-Home.

There will never be satisfactory answer to this man's enigmatic 'wonders', and only Home's reputation as one of the greatest mediums of all time survives. He was alternately praised and vilified in equal measure, but the claim that, amongst other miracles, he floated out of a window several floors above the pavement at Ashley House in London, only to float back in through another window a few moments later, was - according to the witnesses - clear evidence and proof of levitation. Unfortunately, Ashley House is now demolished and all the protagonists are long dead, and therefore their testimony cannot be challenged.

All that can be ascertained is that no-one actually saw him floating outside the building, so what actually happened must of necessity be a matter for conjecture. One Archie Jarman, a member of the Society for Psychical Research (SPR), investigated the case some time later while the building was still standing, and claimed that Home could have achieved the 'levitation' by trickery alone involving ropes and pulleys, (and a good deal of courage it has to be said). This may be so, but like the levitation, his account does not automatically mean that Home, who was also eventually excommunicated by the Catholic Church for sorcery, was a fraud. It is also worth noting that in spite of repeated and closely observed investigations of his abilities, Home was never caught cheating. This is not to say that he did not employ some form of exotic trickery, but if he did then he was a master of his uncanny craft.

The Exorcism of Douglas Deen

One of the most recent, and probably the best known example of exorcism is portrayed in the iconic film mentioned at the beginning, *The Exorcist*. It is informative to learn that the former chief exorcist of the Vatican, Fr. Gabriele Amorth, regards this film as a first class example of what demonic possession is, and how exorcism works. The case on which it is based is also very probably, unlike the first two examples already mentioned, a case of genuine possession. In 1949 a young American boy, Douglas Deen (otherwise known as 'Robbie') began displaying some alarming symptoms and interestingly enough, in common with the case of Nicole Obrey at Luon in medieval France, the family were non-Catholic.

The symptoms afflicting 'Robbie', which included loud noises, furniture spontaneously moving around and his bed shaking violently etc., lasted for several months and persisted through at least two official Catholic Church exorcisms. They were only resolved when, with the family's permission, the boy was eventually baptised into the Catholic faith. On the 18th of April 1949, after enduring four months of possession, Robbie was exorcised in a hospital run by the order of Alexian Brothers. During the ritual, a loud cracking noise was heard that resounded through the hospital and the entity abruptly departed; evidently Robbie was finally and permanently 'cured'.

The reason why the entity should have decided to 'occupy' this young boy appears to have been related to his repeated use of the Ouija board, something an aunt had introduced him to. By using this device, allegedly designed to contact the spirits of the dead, the boy had unwittingly opened a gateway between the dimensions, allowing the invading entity through to take possession of him. Some of these entities, whether infernal or not, are, according to the available information, entirely inimical to humanity in general and continually seek ways to attack us. It is also suggested that it is not the 'soul' that they desire, but instead they act as 'psychic leeches' or 'psychic vampires', feasting on the negative emotions and fear their presence generates in human beings. Whether they are the psychic remnants of the dead is an entirely different question, and one to which there is no easy or ready answer.

Let me be clear about this, I am not for one moment saying that human beings cannot be affected by the non-human and non-corporeal entities that undoubtedly surround us, but what I am saying is that there are groups of people who, although genuine, are seriously misguided. Among the curious aspects of this are the similarities between the symptoms of demonic possession and those of extreme piety and sanctity exhibited by saints and mystics. In both instances (amongst other attributes), the person speaks in languages not known to them, is able to prophesise, can bi-locate (be in two places at once), is able to spontaneously levitate etc., etc. The differences are extremely subtle and evidently require the services of an experienced cleric to discern the difference.

The matter of 'discernment' can be quite controversial and probably extremely subjective, and as we will see this is especially true when dealing with charismatic and evangelical exorcisms. The ability to discern whether or not a person is genuinely demonically possessed is considered to be a gift from spirit, and the person who receives this gift is supposedly an absolute paragon of virtue. As a rule of thumb, if the person becomes ill, starts talking in unknown languages, has feelings of anxiety and depression or has nightmares etc., then the experience is deemed to be demonic in nature.

On the other hand, if the person feels uplifted and experiences visions of God or the saints etc., then the experience must be divine and is therefore blessed. While these judgments may be valid, they are also extremely subjective and arbitrary. This is where the discernment comes in and the person who makes the call has the gifted ability to tell the difference between good and evil. As I already said, this is when the process becomes more than a little subjective and arbitrary.

Chapter 11
Exorcism in the Vatican

One of the most unusual and unlikely settings for an example of exorcism, and perhaps Satanic influence, has to be what should be one of the most revered locations on earth: the sacred fortress that is the Vatican. The source of this information came from two men with intimate knowledge of the Vatican and how it functions. One was the late Malachi Martin, a former Jesuit, sometime exorcist and prolific author, and the other is the previously mentioned Father Gabriel Amorth, the former chief exorcist for the Vatican. Although Fr. Amorth is now retired, he is still one of the most highly regarded and influential of those who administer this rite. According to these two men, not only was there an exorcism conducted in the Vatican, but senior Vatican officials also performed a major rite designed to honour and elevate Lucifer. In addition, several séances have now also been conducted there with the approval of the Holy See.

Actually if one thinks about it, this should come as no real surprise, because various popes compiled books on black magick. Pope Honorious (who created *The Grimoire of Pope Honorious III*, and served as Pope from 1216 until 1227) stands out from the rest due to the horrific nature of the book. This grimoire (or spell book) was one of the most notorious and encyclopaedic works of magick ever assembled. Ostensibly, this was done in order to understand the evil forces the Church was dealing with, and by understanding them deal with and control them more effectively, and some of these forces were presumed to be demons from the deepest pits of Hell.

This still holds true to some degree, and for exactly the same reasons, and applies to clergymen in general and Roman Catholic priests in particular, because, the logic goes, if they can apparently cast out demons in the name of God, then they can control them too. It is also why, in some cases, defrocked or apostate priests were (and still are) reportedly associated with services and rituals designed to bring Satanic entities to this realm. A fair analogy would be a soldier who has been schooled in the arts of war, and who then left the army; the fact that he is no longer in the armed forces does not diminish his training. The same is true of the priesthood, and just because a priest is no longer 'official' does not mean he cannot still use his knowledge and training. The vital difference is that while the soldier (hopefully) should not use his training to kill or maim, what the priest has been taught might be infinitely more dangerous and insidious.

It is very easy for us to dismiss this as nothing more than fanciful (and possibly dangerous) nonsense, but we have to remember that in the Dark Ages, God and Satan were absolutely real. This is not open to question and belief in their reality and the constant war waged between them for the souls of humanity was as real as any of the many wars fought since then. To some extent this was why the long-suffering and fearful public tolerated the ferocious strictures of the Holy Inquisition and the many witch hunts (both Catholic and Protestant) that followed. Violence and brutality was simply part and parcel of daily life, therefore violence in the name of God was just a bit more of the same.

The Vatican Exorcism

As far as the Vatican exorcism went, on September the 6th 2000 towards the end of the regular weekly public audience, a nineteen-year-old woman began screaming and cursing at Pope John Paul II as he moved towards her. The Pope tried blessing her, but to no avail and she had to be restrained by members of the Vatican's security forces. However, the girl seemed to possess remarkable strength and easily threw them off her. Bishop Gianni Danzi then tried to subdue her by placing a crucifix on her, but she just vented her spleen upon him with even more lurid curses. She (or the possessing demon) allegedly also said that, *'not even your church head can send me away'*.

The girl was removed from the crowd to a less public area and Pope John Paul stayed with her for approximately half-an-hour and he promised to say a mass for her the following day, but the effect of the exorcism, his third in twenty-two years (the others were in 1978 and 1982) was temporary. Further investigation revealed that the girl had been possessed since she was twelve-years-old, and in desperation her parents had brought her to the public audience in the hope that she would be helped. Interestingly the girl also became extremely agitated in the presence of any religious iconography. The majority of this account comes from none other than Fr. Gabriel Amorth, who was not present when this example of possession manifested, but he had evidently conducted an exorcism on the girl the previous day. According to the late Cardinal Jacques Martin, the 1982 exorcism conducted by Pope John Paul concerned a woman known only as Francesca F and the invading demon departed from her with little struggle when the Pope agreed to say a mass for her.

Fr. Gabriel Amorth

Fr. Gabriel Amorth is man of considerable fortitude and faith, as he would have to be in his position as the former chief Vatican exorcist and founder and honorary president of the International Association of Exorcists. In his late eighties (as already mentioned he has since retired from that position) he remains as its honorary president for life. Fr. Amorth is not especially upbeat about the prospects of combating the wiles of Satan, and insists - rather worryingly - that an attack on Pope Benedict XVI by a mentally unstable woman on Christmas Eve 2009, plus the accusations of sexual abuse raised against priests in several countries, and the existence of the P2 Masonic Lodge (also called Propaganda Due), are sure signs that, *'The devil resides in the Vatican and you can see the consequences'*. This observation seems to agree with other comments made several years earlier by Pope Paul VI when he said that, *'The Smoke of Satan has found its way into the Church through the fissures'*

While that may or may not be the case, it should come as no surprise to learn that in line with all his courage and certainty in spiritual matters, Fr. Amorth is extremely conservative in his views about the modernisation of the Church. Because he has an obvious vested interest in it, he was especially scathing about the project to translate the traditional *'Rituale Romanum'* form of traditional exorcism from Latin into Italian (and as it happens other languages, including English as well which is the version used in the film *The Exorcist*). He also strenuously argued against the findings of the Vatican II Council (mentioned earlier) when the Latin Mass was substituted for versions using local languages. So his resistance to fundamental changes in the language of the traditional ritual was quite natural.

Fr. Amorth does point out with some justification that of the Cardinals who edited the *'prenotanda'* or introductory texts, none of them had ever actually performed an exorcism or even witnessed one, in other words they did not have clue what they were doing. He also resented the fact that the exorcists working 'on the ground' so to speak were never consulted, but presented with a *fait accompli* once the translation was complete. He also had the impression that the existing exorcists were seen as a negative force acting against the efforts of the modernisers in their opposition to the changes. Fr. Amorth does seem to have a fair point here, because as with the form of words used during transubstantiation being left in their original form because they were, in effect, 'words of inherited power', this could also be said of the words of the Latin version of the *Rituale Romanum*.

Fr. Amorth has, by his own admission conducted literally thousands of exorcisms and according to him those who are genuinely possessed by an evil spirit can, and do, vomit up all sorts of unlikely objects including needles, shards of glass and other small objects. He has commented that even the hierarchy in the Vatican are doubtful that these reports can be genuine and thinks that this all goes to demonstrate that Satan's finest work is convincing people that he does not exist, and that we are all so much the poorer for that. He also bitterly regrets that many countries such as Germany, Switzerland, Spain and Portugal no longer have any officially recognised exorcists.

This may well reflect the increasing embarrassment felt by progressive high-ranking prelates of the Catholic Church who are far from happy when discussing exorcism and possession. Evidently while admitting that it exists, they increasingly believe that it has no place in the modern image the Church wishes to promote. This is a delicate balancing act, because while wishing to modernise, it must be exceedingly difficult to make changes to the fabric that has helped to cement it together for millennia. While Fr. Amorth reports on tales of exorcism and possession occurring inside the walls of the Vatican, Malachi Martin reveals other, perhaps even more worrying, but related, reports from the same location.

Malachi Martin

It has to be said that in some respects the late Malachi Martin was very much in the same mould as Fr. Amorth. Although he left the priesthood and the Jesuits, he still retained the same level of conservative Catholicism and also bitterly resented the changes made during the Vatican II council. This was one of the reasons that he left the Jesuit order, or as he was fond of saying, *'The Jesuits left me'*. The reasons behind his leaving the Jesuits are still rather unclear, but it seems as if he began to question some of the central planks of orthodox belief and he was to some extent shunned by his brethren. This is not to say that they did not at least sympathise with his opinions, but were less inclined to openly question accepted dogma.

Nevertheless he was a well-known and accomplished exorcist and his work in this field is graphically described in his best selling personal factual account, *Hostage to the Devil: The Possession and Exorcism of Five Living Americans,* published in 1975, but the truth, as always, is rather different. Once again we find a faint resonance with *The Exorcist,* because it has to be said that in some ways Malachi Martin resembles the scholarly archaeologist character of Fr. Merrin, one of the two fictional Jesuits, (Fr. Damien Karras SJ was the other). The two Jesuits officiated in the climactic final exorcism that resulted in the removal of the invading demon and the death of both priests, and it has been suggested that Merrin's character was based upon him.

Martin has suggested that a predecessor of Pope Honorious III, the notorious 11th Century Pope Benedict IX, was involved in Satanism and magick and that one of the principle architects of communism, Karl Marx, was also a Satanist. Given the implacable enmity between the Catholic Church and the atheistic ideals at the core of communism this is really not any great surprise. Fr. Martin's mention of Pope Benedict IX is entirely justified and even the Catholic Encyclopaedia describes him as *'A disgrace to the chair of St Peter',* while St Peter Damien describes him as *"A demon from Hell disguised as a priest"* and Pope Victor III talks about his *"Rapes, murders, and other unspeakable acts".* Unusually, according to some sources, Benedict IX was only twelve years of age when he was appointed Pope while others say he was twenty, either way this is remarkably young age at which to attain such a crucial position, so it is likely that there was some political or dynastic move afoot. Another piece of chicanery involving this Pope was when he sold the Papacy to his godfather who took the name Gregory VI.

It is in one of his works of apparent fiction entitled *Windswept House* that the most worrying assertion made by Malachi Martin occurs. In this novel Martin says that on June 29, 1963 a ritual called *'The Enthronement of the Fallen Archangel Lucifer'* was enacted in St. Paul's Chapel in the Vatican, and was linked to concurrent Satanic rites enacted in the U.S.A; all of this took place around eight days after the election of Paul VI. The reason for the ritual conducted in parallel was for the pragmatic reason that to be effective it required sacrifices both animal and human. This would be extremely difficult to conceal in the Vatican, so the sacrifices were carried out in South Carolina in the USA. Apparently this concurrent ritual was, (indeed for it to work it had to be) synchronised to the precise second and both ceremonies were carbon copies of the other.

The ritual in the Vatican was operated by high-ranking prelates and would have automatically rendered them as apostate (denying and rejecting their faith) and what went on the USA was likewise supervised by priests both ordained and otherwise. This act might well be the 'Smoke of Satan' referred to by Pope Paul VI and was supposedly to help usher in the so-called *'Availing Time'*. The term 'Availing Time' relates to a supposed merger of all black magick forces in the world in an act of unity under Satan to create the most powerful magickal convocation ever devised. The choice of St Paul's Chapel is also interesting because this chapel, which is close to the much better known Sistine Chapel, is never open to the public and is used by the Conclave of Cardinals who assemble there when a new Pope is to be elected.

They pray and make their preparations there, then move to the Sistine Chapel to deliberate and vote. St Paul's Chapel also contains two remarkable frescos by Michelangelo that are never normally seen by anyone other than Church officials or Vatican employees. These frescos were completed sometime in the mid 16th Century, and are two of the last (and largest) the old master created. While the Church caused much turmoil and suffering in its history, equally through patronage it was the force behind some of the most spectacularly beautiful and enduring artworks ever created.

Whether or not this ritual actually took place was a bone of contention among those who read the book, and the obvious question was frequently put to Malachi Martin, *viz* was the ritual valid, and did it actually occur as described? At first, perhaps sensing that this could be a real and highly dangerous can of worms, he was equivocal about it, but would not deny it outright. However, shortly before he died in 1999 he was asked again and stated categorically that the novel *Windswept House* was approximately 85% based on hard fact. He also strongly implied that 'The Enthronement of the Fallen Archangel Lucifer' did take place in the manner described and for the purposes stated.

If we take Malachi Martin at his word, then according to the Catholic Church not only are there forces of evil at large in the world, but by association equally there are forces of good. Once again we encounter the Gnostic principles of universal and fundamental balance, yin and yang, high and low, good and evil. The problem is that they seem to merge and converge in one of the few places on the planet capable of keeping a tight rein on them, or perhaps in that environment they cancel one another out, let's hope so. The implications of this are immense because it means that evil (and of course good) are not just abstract concepts, but exist as actual forces that can be harnessed and used. It also seems to authenticate the idea that the beings who are normally assumed to be the products of a much simpler culture, i.e. God, Satan and their cohorts are also real in a literal sense.

The Vatican Séances

It seems rather unsettling to learn that approved séances have also been conducted within the Vatican, and much of what occurred is still a closely guarded secret. From what is known it seems that the idea was the brainchild of Monsignor Ernesto Pisoni, a highly regarded Church official and a former editor of the Catholic newspaper *L'Italia*, and also the author of several books on religion. He has said that his interest in the afterlife was piqued when he began seeing and communicating with the ghost of his deceased brother who died of a heart attack. His communications revealed that his brother was trying to get to 'the light' and that he was in constant pain. Fr. Pisoni took this to refer to the previously mentioned Catholic concept of 'purgatory' where souls that can still be saved are sent to be purified before they finally are accepted into heaven. Evidently, he encountered his brother several times until eventually Fr. Pisoni commented that he became much more peaceful and pain free.

Pisoni is quite adamant that the sprits of the departed are right here and continually moving amongst us, and that there absolutely is a life after death, so he decided to make an official approach to the church to obtain permission to continue his research. He did this, and because the Holy See traditionally disapproved of these practises, he was granted a special dispensation to begin holding séances; the Holy See was as interested as he was in discovering the validity of this research. Apparently, his séances served their purpose and evidence of survival was forthcoming. One experimental séance revealed the presence of a spirit that was buried in unconsecrated ground under the floor of the very building in which they were holding the séance.

After the séance was finished those present went into the cellar and started digging up the floor and a skeleton was uncovered and re-interred shortly after in hallowed ground. Another séance produced a less friendly spirit called 'Gaston' who threatened to kill them all. Pisoni reports that furniture in the room started to shake and pictures fell off the wall. 'Gaston' told them that while drunk he had murdered his wife and children using a hatchet. The priest claims to have checked out this information and found evidence that 'Gaston' was French, and was a known criminal with violent tendencies and that he had indeed killed his family. Unfortunately Monsignor Pisoni does not reveal whether or not a medium was used, nor the type of séance for there are several, and once again we have to take this at face value.

What does become clear though is that the Catholic Church does have an extremely keen interest in matters relating to the spirit and its survival after death, and it obviously takes the matter of demonic interference in the daily lives of human beings as a matter of real concern. While its desire to keep up with continually changing cultural morals can be viewed as positive, it might also have unexpected side effects in the long term, and perhaps Fr. Amorth's intransigence is right, and change for the sake of change is not a good idea. This is a trend seen in many areas of public and private life and might even be a contributing factor in the continuing implosion of western values and traditions.

Chapter 12
The Faith Movement Inheritance

I n order to set all of this in some kind of present day context we should begin with a look a how much of the present situation came into being, and that means the creation of 'The Faith Movement'. To fully explore this idea would require a book in itself, so we will have to content ourselves with a condensed version, but it will be sufficient to allow us at least a basic understanding of how this contentious doctrine functions. First came the teachings of Phineas Parkhurst Quimby, the founder of the 'New Thought' movement who became interested in the techniques first developed by Frantz Mesmer (creator of Mesmerism) and from this developed a reputation as something of a healer. He also came to believe that sickness and disease were attributable to 'improper thinking', and that humans had the ability to heal themselves by positive thinking, or 'affirmation' as he and his followers called it.

All that was required was for the sufferer to verbalise their wishes, and if they were sufficiently devout they could alter or 'edit' reality to allow this to happen. From these beginnings arose such organisations as 'Religious Science' founded in 1927 by Earnest Holmes, the 'Christian Scientists' founded in 1879 by Mary Baker Eddy, and 'The Unity School of Christianity' founded in 1889 by Charles and Myrtle Fillmore. All of these pseudo-religions (which still exist) obviously have variations in what they teach, and how they teach it, but they are all united by one central tenet. This is that we can directly affect and interact with the world we live in and cause change, especially regarding our health, to occur by merely wishing (praying) for it to be so.

While this is all well and good in relation to Godly pursuits, it also carries about it considerably more than a whiff of how magick supposedly operates, something, however, that would be complete anathema to the preachers. Evidently God does not want us to be ill or in pain, so a suitable invocation will ensure that our illnesses are cured. However, while the Unity School does not reject conventional medicine, the Christian Scientists do, to the point of refusing blood transfusions etc., and this has led to the deaths of many of its adherents. The Christian Scientists, or 'The Church of Christ Scientist' as it is more correctly known, and its practitioners are quite happy to help those who are ill through what they define as, 'the false reality of illness', which, by definition, seems to be an extremely risky process. Unless an illness is entirely psychosomatic or a pretence, then it is anything but a 'false reality'.

This, or certain precepts of it, developed separately into the theology practised by those who preach the gospel according to the Faith Movement using exactly the same basic techniques, but for much more base and venal proposes. One main difference is that rather than attribute what they are doing to the power of the mind, they much prefer to attribute it to the 'force of faith'. To be fair here, the act of faith and what it can achieve (and has achieved) may well be the most powerful example of what the mind can do and this may have relevance to a variety of otherwise inexplicable phenomena attributed to various saints. One writer from the 'New Thought' movement, Warren Felt Evans, encapsulated this rather neatly when he said, *'The effect of the suggestion is the result of the faith of the subject, for it is always proportioned to the degree in which the patient believes what you say'*. This is 100% correct and it can be very difficult to see why those who attribute the cures to God cannot see that, if nothing else, God may need a little help and cooperation from the patient.

The Faith Movement stalwarts like Kenneth Copeland, (more of whom later) and Kenneth Hagen promote individuals like William Branham, one of the Pentecostalist founders of the post WWII faith healing movement, as icons within their own organisations. However, like many of his ilk, Branham was rabidly anti-Catholic to the point of denying the validity of the Holy Trinity, which he said was a Satanic concept. He also claims that he heard God talking to him from an early age right up until a defining moment in 1933. While baptising converts in the Ohio river, people standing on the bank told him that a shining light hovered above him while a voice told him that, *'As John the Baptist was sent to forerun the first coming of Jesus Christ, so your message will forerun His second coming.'*

He took this as total vindication of his ministry and like many others with a similar world view, developed a talent for healing (and evidently to some extent telepathy) in that he seemed to know what the afflicted person who approached him during his many spiritual renewal crusades was thinking. Again like many of his kind Branham was also given to making prophesies, although he called them predictions, this supposed talent was never really a good idea, especially when his statement that 1977 would terminate all world systems and usher in the millennium was proven wrong. This did not greatly affect him though because he died 12 years earlier in 1965; it did not diminish the faith of his followers either who still regard him as one of the great evangelists.

Another forerunner was the old-time, barnstorming, tub-thumping Pentecostal preacher/healer/miracle worker Asa A. Allen (A.A Allen) who, as well as running a highly successful and extremely lucrative ministry, died of acute liver failure brought about by chronic alcoholism. His greatest claim to fame was probably that he could command God to turn one-dollar bills into twenties. His successor was Don Stewart who took over the ministry and continued on the same lines. We shall also encounter the Rev Stewart, who also promotes miracles on demand through a 'green prayer handkerchief', again a little later.

While on the subject of remarkable claims we should consider another of the icons of fundamentalism and charismatic ministry that is Oral Roberts. The Rev Roberts claimed that God personally told him that his mission was to find the cure for cancer and that he should build a 'research tower' to do this. On the basis of God's received instructions he sent out an appeal saying that God told him, *'I would not have had you and your partners build the 20 storey research tower unless I was going to give you a plan to attack cancer'*. The money was duly collected and the tower built, but it was later sold off to property developers and as one might expect no cure for cancer was found. The Rev Roberts still carries his message on a regular basis through the God channels of satellite television, although it is unclear whether he still receives advice and instruction directly from God.

Although the mainstream Protestant religions officially stopped conducting exorcisms approximately twenty five years ago, this is not true of the smaller fundamentalist, charismatic and Pentecostal churches, especially in the United States of America, that never abandoned the rite. In these organisations the ritual of systematic exorcism is actively encouraged even when there are no obvious signs of possession; it is almost looked upon as a rite-of-passage when a newcomer joins the congregation and these rituals often involve several people at one time.

The pastors and exorcists actively encourage those who may or may not be possessed by demons and other entities to bellow, scream, writhe on the floor, recant and purge themselves of whatever entity they believe is within them. This sometimes queasy procedure regularly ends with personal injury, trauma and projectile vomiting. Such is the strength of belief that those undergoing exorcism believe that adultery, alcoholism, laziness, overeating, tiredness and a host of mundane, and not so mundane, conditions are directly attributable to 'demonic forces'.

Whether the ritual is effective due to spiritual cleansing or for purely psychosomatic reasons is difficult to judge, but the practice appears to add a measure of 'glamour' to the version of Christian religion on offer. The ebullient and thrusting style of charismatic and evangelical Christianity may even create the atmosphere where imagined manifestations of evil can flourish and snare the unwary or insufficiently devout. Although it serves the purposes of those running the religious group, to the outsider it carries more than a hint of hucksterism and charlatanry.

We started out looking at cases of traditional religious exorcism and associated phenomena, and as a result find ourselves drawn into some of the almost freakish sideshows that have become associated with this. Modern times produce modern claims and unfortunately none more astonishing and unlikely than those made by certain televangelists who claim not only to drive out demons and 'slay in the spirit', but to raise the dead. Yes, they channel so much spiritual energy and power direct from God Himself that they can raise the dead, and that is a claim that even the most ardent medieval priest, bishop or pope could not, and would not, make.

They, as with the church-appointed exorcists, claim the ability to cast out demons due to the fact that Christ drove out demons and that they only emulate this ability by assuming the same mantle. In fact Jesus Christ was probably the most important of all the exorcists and His abilities (which he passed on to his disciples, in other words he 'anointed' them) are mentioned specifically in scripture. In Mark 1:39 we find that *'Jesus preached and cast out devils'* and in Acts 19:12 *'Jesus rebuked the foul spirit saying unto him, thou deaf and dumb spirit I charge thee come out of him and enter no more into him and the sprit cried and rent him sore and came out of him'*.

There are at least a further twenty scriptural examples of this including one where, while exorcising a madman, (again the mentally ill are assumed to be demonically possessed) Jesus commands the demons into a herd of swine who ran over a cliff and drowned in the waters below. This seems to hark to the fate of the previously mentioned father Damien Karras in *The Exorcist*, when he took the invading entity into his body then promptly leaped to his death on the steeply banked stone stairway beneath the upstairs bedroom window of the possessed child.

Because Jesus was an exorcist and wielded the power of God and transferred his gifts to his disciples, several modern televangelists make the assumption that by association that includes them too and one in particular, Pastor Benny Hinn, a charismatic evangelical American who heads up Benny Hinn Ministries (BHM), makes these dangerous claims. Before proceeding, I should make clear that I am not religious and other than the methods he employs have no particular issue with the Rev Hinn, he is one many similar evangelists, but is perhaps more outrageous than the rest.

In fact Benny Hinn makes many astonishing assertions, he even went so far as to claim on the 'Trinity Broadcasting Network' (TBN) that if the dead were brought in their coffins and placed beside a TV set during one of his sermons, the power of God would come through the TV and awaken them and restore them to life. Again on TBN he made what constitutes a direct threat: *"I place a curse on every man and woman that will stretch his hand against this anointing. I curse that man who dares to speak a word against this ministry. But any man, [or] any woman that raises his or her hand in blessing toward this ministry, I bless that man...."*

Some clarification might be required here; 'the anointing' referred to by Hinn is a phenomenon, which he claims was given to him directly by God, and allows him to heal. This talent for healing has, he claims, allowed him to heal everything from cancer to AIDS and, significantly, severe physical injuries. Again in relation to his anointing, he used to visit the graves of Katherine Kuhlman and Aimee Semple McPherson, both (for their time) extremely media savvy Pentecostalists and faith healers, to obtain further 'anointing' from their bones, something that carries more than a hint of distaste and queasiness about it.

Some more of pastor Hinn's remarkable claims bear closer scrutiny. One such statement suggested that the east coast of America would experience a massive and destructive earthquake at some point during the 1990s. Another was that 'The Rapture', when the faithful, (again in the 1990s) would be raised up bodily into heaven to remain with God until 'The Tribulation' ended, and the Godless would be slain in a series of ferocious wars.

The pastor rather craftily added the rider that this was guaranteed to occur within the next two years...unless of course Jesus/the Lord changed His mind. When discussing The Rapture and its supposed effects it is as well to consider what supposedly occurred to the few saints (and others) mentioned later in the book who displayed spiritual phenomena such as stigmata and spontaneous levitation etc. There are several descriptions of particularly focussed individuals, although perhaps obsessive would be a better term, of being in a trance or 'rapture' and levitating at various heights in the air. Might this be a reference to the same effect?

In 1997 during a fundraising telethon on TBN he assured us that Jesus would return in the next two years. In addition to this he laid out his stall quite clearly when he said *'I don't need gold in heaven, I need it now'*. One of the most outrageous, almost comical, claims was that since Adam had dominion over the 'fowls of the air', this meant that he could fly. After all, if he had dominion over birds then he could obviously fly and in fact with one thought he could fly to the moon...truly remarkable (and nonsensical) stuff indeed! As far as healing goes, the heavyweight boxer Evander Holyfield once attended one of Hinn's healing crusades in Pennsylvania after being prevented from boxing due to an apparent heart condition. The indefatigable pastor laid hands on him and graciously received a cheque for $265,000 when he pronounced Holyfield cured.

Much to his delight the boxer went on to pass a subsequent medical examination arranged by the boxing commission: proof indeed! However, it later emerged that the boxer had never had a heart condition in the first place, he had been misdiagnosed, but this was almost certainly regarded by Hinns apologists as the work of Satan trying to deflect the appropriate praise for the work of the Lord. It is unclear if the cheque was ever returned. On a rather poignant note, during one of his regular healing and fundraising crusades, this time in Canada, when a woman tried to bring her daughter who suffered from Muscular Dystrophy to have her blessed by the pastor, his minders turned her away. In fact any of those who attend his Crusades looking for relief or healing and suffer from an obvious affliction, or are seriously mentally handicapped, never make it to the stage. This rather tends to make his outrageous claims less than provable, and both cynical and distasteful.

As far as fund raising is concerned, in 2007 BHM sent out fundraising fliers to the faithful to purchase a luxurious Gulfstream G4SP 22 seat private aircraft (which cost $36 million to buy and around $600,000 per year to operate and maintain). The fundraising must have been successful because an aircraft named 'Dove One' was duly purchased from the donations of a minimum $1,000 per head. Mind you, for this you were promised (predictably) that wealth would be bestowed upon you, and you also got a plaque with your name on it placed in the aircraft. This sounds suspiciously like another similar ministry making claims made for what it called the so-called 'faith seed'. This extolled the benefits to be had by sending in money (a 'faith seed') which would be miraculously transformed by the Lord into material benefits for the donor.

I should add that the Rev Hinn is not the only one doing this and these wild and specious claims are also made by similar organisations fuelled by literalist, overheated interpretations of scripture. A leisurely scan of the previously mentioned God Channels on satellite television provides prime examples of utterly jaw-dropping viewing. In truth, scandalous assertions like these serve the Christian - and indeed all - churches ill, and the often affluent lifestyles frequently adopted by these multi-millionaire, self-styled evangelists and prophets even more so. Ron Hubbard who invented 'Scientology' once said that the best way to make money was to found a religion...he was right of course, it still is.

Before leaving the works of Pastor Hinn and his BHM organisation, it would be churlish not to mention the fact that they (and of course the other ministries) do actually give a percentage of the money they receive to the poor, the needy and those afflicted by natural disasters. According to figures released by BHM, they support around 60 missions around the world, and also feed and care for 100,000 children per year. In addition to this they evidently they provide 200,000 patients with free medical care. This makes it even harder to accept the wilder statements made by Rev Hinn and of course his overtly lavish lifestyle. In 1997 BHM was taking in around $60 million per year (not all that big by evangelical standards) and Hinn's personal income was anywhere between $500,000 and £1 million per year.

Evangelism and Witchcraft

We should also consider that in some parts of the United Kingdom there are variants on this type of theology fast growing in the inner cities, mainly in the black community.

The appointment of Britain's first black Archbishop of York, the Rev John Sentamu, was an attempt to control the more than one hundred listed breakaway black evangelical churches in the London area alone. These evangelical churches have an appalling record on spurious exorcisms, the 'Kendocki' strain of witchcraft, human rights abuses and the consumption of "bushmeat". Bushmeat is derived from both human and animal carcasses and various body parts are smuggled into Britain, mostly from Africa, for use in witchcraft or for delicacies. Eighty Kendocki murders were registered in Nigeria alone last year, and according to the British police many of these body parts ended up in Britain. Just what the consumption of bushmeat has to do with Christian traditions is unclear, unless it is a literal interpretation of Christ's instruction about 'eating his body and blood'.

On October the 4th 2005 Britain's Charity Commission condemned one breakaway Christian church for "serious misconduct and mismanagement". A subsequent investigation revealed that pastor Matthew Ashimolowo, the head of London's *"Kingsway International Christian Centre"* (KICC) used church funds to purchase an £80,000 car. £120,000 was spent on drink and prostitutes for a 'religious party', and £13,000 on a time-share in Florida. The prosecution was successful and resulted in the pastor agreeing to repay £300,000 back to the church. The pastor is a Pentecostalist who still regularly appears on the TBN channels, and used the notorious affront of Prosperity Theology to justify his £100,000 per year salary.

His church has assets of over £22.9 million with a mainly poor, black afro-Caribbean congregation. According to the pastor he sees no dichotomy in the size of the assets, his salary (or those of his directors who earn between £60,000 and £80,000 per year) and the relative poverty of his congregation. The KICC director of finance, Soji Otudeko, said that *"People give because of how they have been blessed by what they receive from the church, the teaching, the prayer and the church community. People give voluntarily and because of their love of the work of God."*

Whether through shame, unease or maybe even guilty conscience, the pastor eventually took heed of the adverse publicity and stepped down, and the new chief operating officer is a former oil executive James McGlashan. McGlashan insists that the church preaches self-development and if that means wealth then so be it. Another Nigerian operating in the same area is Bishop David Oyedepo, one of the wealthiest pastors in Nigeria, who heads Ministries International Inc, which in turn also flourishes in other countries under the name of *'Winners Chapel'* and *'Living Faith Church'*. We will look at Prosperity Theology in the next chapter.

As a footnote to this whole rather nauseating saga we should take a brief and final look at Kenneth Copeland to see just how divorced from reality these characters really are. One of Copeland's worst and truly breathtaking utterances refers directly to Jesus Christ, the person whose teachings he is supposedly promoting. Almost incredibly, Copeland announced that God was the greatest failure of all time and that Satan conquered Jesus on the cross. As if this was not bad enough, he also described Christ in Hell as, *"An emaciated, poured out, little wormy spirit"*. Irrespective of the context in which this was said, these words cannot ever be acceptable and are more suited to the likes of the late Anton LaVey the founder of 'The Church of Satan', who for obvious reasons regularly decried Christ and everything He stood for.

One of his books in particular, *The Satanic Bible* is full of observations and homilies about the need to lash out against the timidity and humility of religious and biblical teachings, and accept the supposed freedom and sheer joy of Satanism. Again hardly acceptable, but at least people - although they might find the philosophy repugnant - knew what LaVey was and what he stood for, plus he could at least justify what he said in the context of his beliefs, while Copeland does not even have a fig leaf to hide behind. This should be enough to put any self respecting Christian believer right off any message he tries to convey, but evidently he still has his followers.

It should serve as some kind of further warning about others of a similar ilk to learn that none other than Benny Hinn said in support of this man that, *'Those who attack Kenneth Copeland are attacking the very presence of God'*. In common with pastor Benny Hinn *et al*, Copeland also vigorously preaches deliverance, casting out devils, and prosperity theology, and again like Hinn was 'anointed' by the Holy Spirit. On first sight it appears that it may not have been anything divine that 'anointed' these men, and their dubious calling may have been directed from the opposite end of the spiritual spectrum.

Chapter 13
Pentecostalists and Charismatics

I n this book there have been many references to various shades of religion and religious belief but, for reasons stated at the beginning, the single most prevalent one is that of Christianity. As far as deliverance ministry goes, the most significant and influential amongst this particular strain of belief have been Pentecostalists and Charismatics, and although Charismatic behaviour can be found within the Roman Catholic Church, for the purposes of the book I will concentrate on the Protestant beliefs. It is important that we do so because it helps make sense of contextualise much of what is written here because a considerable body of work has been written about them and their theology. It is obviously an extremely complex issue, so once again for reasons of space and clarity I do not intend to explore every nook and cranny.

However the fact that the exponents of these beliefs consider themselves to have been 'filled', 'baptised', or in some cases 'anointed' by a spiritual source must surely amount to something very close to possession. Does it also therefore follow that the legitimate ceremony of baptism as practised in a Christian church, especially the Roman Catholic Church, allowing the concept of 'original sin' to be expunged is also a form of exorcism? The idea of original sin in non-baptised infants that would have automatically have had them condemned to purgatory has in recent years been rethought by the Catholic Church, which now says that this would not happen to an otherwise innocent baby.

Pentecostalists

The idea behind the Pentecostal and Charismatic movement lies in the evangelical interpretation of the Bible, which in itself finds resonances with what came to be called 'The Great Awakening'. This first Great Awakening (there have arguably been four of these, the last supposedly in the late 1960s) manifested during the early 18th Century in the United States of America, and is seen by some as a precursor to the American Revolution. Ministers such as the Rev George Whitefield sought to involve their flocks into understanding the implications and power represented by scripture and encouraged them to react spontaneously and emotionally to anything they found especially enlightening or exciting.

Evangelicals, to fully embrace their calling, have to become spiritually 'born again' in scripture using the quotation, *'That which is born of the flesh is flesh; and that which is born of the Spirit is spirit. Marvel not that I said unto thee, ye must be born again" (John 3:1-7)* as justification for their beliefs. They are often at great pains to distance themselves from bible literalists and fundamentalists, but the differences are often very difficult to discern. That said, it is an excellent example of how scripture can be used to justify myriad nuances and vagaries of just about any belief system. Not surprisingly on that basis there are many variants on Christian belief, each absolutely certain that they are correct, all of whom use scripture to justify their stance. It is unlikely that they can all be correct, but that is true of all religion.

Pentecostals, who derive their beliefs directly for the above source, embrace the idea of 'spiritual renewal'. However, with the added refinement of *'Baptism in the Holy Spirit'* in commemoration of when the spirit of Christ descended on his remaining eleven disciples (Judas had hanged himself in guilt at his betrayal) and 'anointed' them with the power to speak in His name and display magickal gifts like healing etc. Some groups of Pentecostals accept the Holy Trinity of Father, Son and Holy Spirit, while others vehemently do not. This is why these particular sub-schisms are often fervently and almost incoherently anti-Catholic to the point of denouncing the Pope as either the anti-Christ or Satan. They also frequently depict the Catholic religion as Satanically inspired. As one would expect, they can also justify this through reference to their interpretation of scripture. As far as being baptised in the Holy Spirit is concerned, this is a deeply personal experience and involves repentance of all sin and the reality of being born again and spiritually renewed. The baptism can be halted or delayed if the person asking for it does so out of 'impure motives' (i.e. financial gain which should, but clearly does not, rule out all of those preaching the scandalous message of prosperity theology) or their belief is too weak. When the blessing does occur it imbues the recipient with the ability to 'speak in tongues' (also called glossolalia) and the mostly incoherent sounds made are said to be the Holy Spirit speaking through the person.

The incoherence is due to the lack of ability or capacity in a human being to properly articulate the sheer power and magnitude of this force. In addition, those so blessed can supposedly understand other languages that should be unknown to them and have the gift of prophesy, and in some instances healing too. Importantly, the spirit baptism also gifts them the ability, as with the disciples, to discern demons and evil spirits and if necessary cast them out. This is perhaps one of the most important and contentious issues in the whole canon of Pentecostal teaching because it also infringes on at least one aspect of the subjects they abhor, i.e. the Roman Catholic Church and its rite of exorcism.

Speaking in Tongues

It is worth looking at the phenomenon of glossolalia in some detail because it is one of the central planks of Pentecostalism. The gift of speaking in tongues or *'glossolalia'* (from the Greek, 'glosso') has been known for millennia. It is recorded in the New Testament by St Paul and St Luke in Acts 2:1-42 that speaking in tongues was a regular part of life in the early Christian church. According to them, when the Holy Spirit descended at Pentecost following the first Easter, it imparted this gift to the faithful, *"On the day of Pentecost, the apostles began to speak in tongues"*.

The glossolalia as performed in most Pentecostal and charismatic churches is completely incomprehensible unless some other member of the congregation is able to interpret it. This still occurs to this day in Pentecostal services because the person in the ecstatic trance still cannot be understood. One scientific description of the phenomenon states; *"Glossolalia i.e. speaking in tongues is vocalisation that sounds like language, but is devoid of semantic meaning or syntax. In the Christian tradition, this vocalisation pattern is associated with possession by the Holy Spirit and communication directly with God through prayer or prophecy. Some scientific investigators conceptualise glossolalia as the product of an altered or disassociated state of consciousness, whereas others view it as symptomatic of psychopathology"* [**Science Frontiers** #51, May-June, © 1987-2000 William R Corliss].

The main biblical justification for speaking in tongues occurs throughout the epistle to the Corinthians, and in the King James Bible we find: *'For he that speaketh in an unknown tongue speaketh not to man, but unto God: for no man understands him; howbeit in the spirit he speaketh mysteries'*. This is also mentioned in Mark 16:17 *'These signs will accompany those who have believed: In my name they will cast out demons, they will speak with new tongues'*. Rather more straightforwardly, the Bible in basic English says: *'For he who makes use of tongues speaks not to men, but to God; because no one has the sense of what he is saying: but in the spirit he is saying secret things'*

Other sects also claim the ability to speak in tongues, examples have also occurred while performing "The Toronto Blessing", which is another form of Pentecostalism. Another rather disconcerting aspect of this is its connection to the occult and Tantric concept of 'Kundalini', or how human beings might connect with subtle energies derived from universal consciousness. It is difficult to see how this would have any attraction to fundamentalist Christianity, but as with many aspects of spirituality the methods employed to achieve the necessary states of ecstasy are virtually identical.

In the instance of the Toronto Blessing, the glossolalia is expressed as laughter and barking. In other examples of Pentecostalism the experiencer normally, although not exclusively, stands immobile, their face in a beatific expression and allows a string of repetitive sounds to escape from their mouths. As is the case in other examples of similar states, when someone starts vocalising, the condition tends to spread to others in the congregation. The people experiencing this ecstatic state are, for their own safety, usually watched over by others not directly participating in the experience. Sometimes the 'language' devolves into tears and laughter; but from a non-partisan standpoint the utterances are gibberish. Might this 'group effect' find resonances with what occurred to the possessed nuns at the Loudon?

To be fair, having observed this phenomenon at first hand it is initially rather unsettling. It is difficult to put the sounds into words, but during my encounter they sounded like, *"Leedle addle eedle eedle oodle oddle addle addle addle"*. This stream of similar word-like sounds was repeated like a mantra until the celebrant finally came out of their trance, or perhaps some sort of ecstatic state. This is typical of the 'words' produced by those involved in the ceremonies; they may vary slightly, but are always like words, although never lucid sentences. On the other hand, speaking conventional languages that are unknown to the experiencer is an entirely different experience and rather more difficult to explain, this is known as xeno-glossolalia and is often found in people who are supposedly possessed by evil spirits.

This seems to suggest that there is a link here and that something very fundamental is occurring. It has been noted at rallies and 'crusades' organised by the previously mentioned Pastor Benny Hinn that the Rev Hinn often strides back and forth in front of his audiences while 'speaking in tongues' and his eager congregations sways, eyes closed and arms raised apparently entranced. Whether or not this is part of his flamboyant style of preaching remains to be seen, as does evidence that it is not entirely for the benefit of the crowd. One thing that is certain, is that it is deeply embarrassing to watch, but it does encourage the crowd to dig deep in their pockets when the collection is taken.

However, it is still possible that the person who actually does speak in a genuine foreign language has been in contact either with someone who actually spoke the language or heard it while on holiday and absorbed it into the subconscious. One of the scientific explanations for this is:

> *'Glossolalia is a psycholingual catharsis. Entering into an uncontrolled, spontaneous, energetic verbal creativity, it seems reasonable that a great variety of sounds could ensue. Temporarily detached from a conscious connection to his or her natural language, the vocal tract of the glossolalist is allowed to contort into otherwise unfamiliar positions. This does not mean that glossolalia would be any less language-like. It would mean however that speaking in tongues is closer to a schizophrenic's 'word salad' than a divine language. Research has shown that both 'schizophrenese' and faked glossolalia to be much less 'language-like' than the real thing.'* [©2000 Institute for First Amendment Studies, Inc]

Perhaps so, but where does this leave us regarding the reality of speaking in tongues as a genuine manifestation of spirit? It is understood that the argument put forward by Pentecostalists, and other sects who use glossolalia, states that it is a message from the Holy Spirit channelled through man. However, perhaps the final word on this belongs to William Samarin, a long time researcher into glossolalia.

> *"When the full apparatus of linguistic science comes to bear on glossolalia, this turns out to be only a façade of a language – although at times a very good one indeed. For when we comprehend what language is, we must conclude that no glosso, no matter how well constructed, is a specimen of human language, because it is neither internally organised nor systematically related to the world man perceives".* [Ibid]

Glossolalia is not confined to Christian Pentecostalists and saints; the origins of this manifestation predate Christianity and are seen in Judaic, Buddhist, Hindu and Islamic mysticism, and the function is identical. In Islamic mystical teaching (Sufism), when the utterances are produced only the sounds change, in this instance it is called *'Shathiyat'* or mystical utterance, which may occur whilst in an ecstatic state. While there is no intention to debunk practitioners of Christian or non-Christian fundamentalist belief systems, there appears to be a great deal of peer pressure involved to deliver the voice of the Holy Spirit.

Because the framework of the ceremonies and initiation rites are designed to create suitable conditions for the phenomena to occur, the individual celebrant may feel he or she is required to produce proof of their sincerity. This 'madness of crowds syndrome' is something often seen in the rambunctious and chaotic Pentecostal deliverance ministry exorcisms. The vocalisations invariably tend to follow simple, meaningless, repetitive patterns than can be interpreted to mean anything the listener chooses. Biblical justifications aside, of all the alleged physical phenomena associated with mysticism, glossolalia is too easily faked and open to misinterpretation, and is unlikely to be held valid except by those who choose to accept it.

The ability to sense the presence of demons, and of course to prophesise, is also one of the talents displayed by psychic mediums and channellers (in this case there is no difference because the ability functions in exactly the same way). Anyone who displays these abilities is tapping into a reservoir of, let's call it 'power', and its use depends on who is using it and why it is used. Those who use it for the benefit of Pentecostal causes must by association be deemed holy, pious or, even better, 'righteous' and therefore acting for the greater glory of God, the common good, or at least for the benefit of their beliefs. On the other hand, mediums - irrespective of whether they use it to help or reassure someone in great need - are automatically using conventional religious standards. What tends to be quite remarkable here is the parallel paths that magickal abilities confer on those who are given them.

Charismatic beliefs

There are striking similarities between these two variants of the same schism of belief with very little or no differences between those who espouse Pentecostal beliefs and their Charismatic siblings. The idea behind Charismatic Christianity, which also uses speaking in tongues to demonstrate its commitment, began in the 1960s as a direct offshoot of Pentecostalism and was confined mainly, but not exclusively, to the middle classes again in the USA. It suited the conservative mindset of the middle class because the wilder excesses of the Pentecostalists were regarded as much too flamboyant and unrestrained for their sensibilities.

From a purely pragmatic perspective it did not really matter since there was a religious reward of renewal at the end of it, and it is this strain of Christianity that was hijacked by the many televangelists as their ticket to wealth and salvation accompanied by signs, wonders and miracles. What also singles out Charismatic belief as special is the fact that it is, unlike many other 'off message' beliefs, enthusiastically endorsed by the Roman Catholic Church and there are several Charismatic Catholic centres dotted all over the world.

Chapter 14
Prosperity Theology and the Faith Movement

The televangelists will almost guarantee that through them God will make you rich; actually cause money to come your way. Don Stewart and Rod Parsley, also Americans, are in the main, but by no means the only, proponents of these fatuous and unlikely claims. The really tragic thing is that they can legally do this and on a daily basis too, on the aforementioned God Channels. They might even be genuine in their beliefs, but raising the dead and God paying your bills? No, that did not, does not and will not happen, except in the minds of dubious TV evangelists and in the earnest wishes and desires of the well intentioned, but gullible, members of the public.

It is especially depressing in these financially straitened times that groundless claims like this seem ever more tempting. Bear in mind that none of this is free; absolutely none of it and for God to reward you with money you need to plant a 'faith seed', which of course means send in money to the evangelist. Pastor Hinn, who we have already encountered, does not say whether or not you can pay to be raised from the dead, but the other two are quite clear that in return for money God will reward you literally...and handsomely. While researching the book I contacted one of these ministries and asked if it was possible to obtain a refund if the promised wealth did not materialise. I said that since God was the guarantor then this had to be a certainty, so a refund should be no problem. Unfortunately, this was not part of the deal, so I did not take up the offer of free money.

It is difficult to choose from the many who espouse these beliefs, but one last example of this comes in the form of yet another televangelist (there are dozens of them), this time a woman - for the field is very much open to all - called Joyce Myer. The Rev Dr Myer is also in the ranks of the super-rich through her advocacy of Prosperity Theology where God makes you rich, in fact God actively WANTS you to be rich...but obviously at a cost. Dr Myer at least does not pretend otherwise and openly and shamelessly brags that God made her rich, very rich indeed, and God also supplied the private jet that takes her from place to place preaching her version of the gospel.

This is said with no hint of embarrassment either, and everything she possesses in terms of material goods came from Him as a reward for her abundant depth of faith. Presumably as well as the jet aircraft, that reward includes her husband's expensive silver Mercedes car, her $2 million home plus all the luxurious furnishings and four more houses worth another $2 million for each of her children. The houses are actually part of a family compound bought by Joyce Myer Ministries containing a total of five dwellings, all built to very high standards and all luxurious. All expenses, including landscaping the homes and their running costs etc., are paid for by the Ministry, and the good reverend and her family live there free...nice! It is as well to mention that the cost of the expensive TV shows is also met by her supporters.

Once again we should pause to examine the drivers behind Prosperity Theology and the Faith Movement, i.e. the interpretation of scripture that created it, a little more thoroughly. Not, you understand, that it will make any difference to those who shamelessly enjoy its benefits nor, sadly, to those who misguidedly choose to contribute to it. The idea of this almost uniquely American take on the Bible and scripture has been compared to the activities of cults that have grown up around various strands of biblical teaching, and surely reflects poorly on those who preach it and the otherwise empty lives of those who follow them. It seems as if there will always be individuals who need to find salvation by any means.

These are all blessings, says Dr Myer, bestowed straight from the hand of God. Let's face it, if God is going to bestow riches then why would He be a cheapskate, oh yes...only the very best for His chosen ones. One is forced to ask whether they serve God or money, or maybe they no longer know the difference ... although there is ample said about it in the book whose wisdom they claim to follow. The King James Version puts it like this in Matthew 6:24: *"No man can serve two masters: for either he will hate the one, and love the other; or else he will hold to the one, and despise the other. Ye cannot serve God and mammon."* In this case, Mammon was an ancient deity of wealth and property worshipped by the Sumerians and was co-opted along with much else into the Bible.

Evidently, these earnest custodians of the gospel can justify what they do by judicious referencing of other quotes from the same book: shame on them! To justify their avaricious take on scripture they are quick to point out that Jesus and his disciples were apparently men of some substance who travelled for three years with no obvious means of support. They met and socialised with wealthy people and Jesus had a treasurer (Judas Iscariot), a choice that makes one wonder if this was in some way included as an afterthought to make sure that Judas was somehow apart from the rest. Actually all of these interpretations seem strangely at odds with the other biblical portrayals of Christ.

Lastly, since we mentioned Ron Hubbard and wealth we might as well look briefly at the Scientologists: The late Ron Hubbard who invented Scientology in 1953 (four years after saying *'I'd like to start a religion, that's where the money is'*)...was right and duly became a multi-millionaire. However, one thing that Scientology does not do is make wild claims about the favours granted by any creator God since it does not accept the traditional concept of God in the first place...although it does allow for a 'supreme being'. Those wishing to advance through the levels of this self-styled 'religion' do so by paying handsomely for a series if pre-packaged modules of psychological programming to attain the ultimate secret of the extraterrestrial origins of the human race...and that of course does not involve God in any way at all.

Actually Hubbard had an ambivalent relationship with religion and its close cousin, magick, and it is known that at one point he was involved with the rocket scientist and magician Jack Parsons (one of the founders of the Jet Propulsion Laboratory in Pasadena, California) when the two of them attempted to operate the *'Babalon Working'* to create a 'moonchild'. The ritual (Liber49) was devised by Parsons, and based heavily on the much earlier Thelemic work of Aleister Crowley, whom he knew. The intention of the ritual was the creation of a 'magickal child' in the astral plain, and have it born via a surrogate mother (Marjorie Cameron) here on earth. At any rate Hubbard and Parsons attempted the ritual, which Hubbard finally brought to a halt by claiming it a success.

No child was apparently born, although Parsons did eventually marry Marjorie Cameron. Scientologists claim that Hubbard, who they say was in naval intelligence, was only monitoring the activities of Parsons in the interests of US national security. All that is certain here is that Hubbard was in the US Marine Corps and did briefly command two anti-submarine vessels, but was removed from command because he was not judged capable. Hubbard (and of course the Scientologists) claim a much more glowing and illustrious career and that the US Navy deliberately altered his records to discredit him.

Oddly enough Aleister Crowley, although he never met him, disliked Hubbard intensely and denounced him as a fraud and conman. This judgement was apparently justified when Hubbard absconded with Parsons' then girlfriend and a sum of cash supposedly to further a business deal, and embarked on a cruise. It may seem odd that we have taken this apparent diversion away from the more obvious manifestations of religion (albeit outré), but when looked at dispassionately it soon becomes obvious that there is little or no difference between religion and magick, especially when supernatural forces are invoked to drive out demons, heal the sick, perform miracles...or create magickal children.

Chapter 15
A Very British Exorcist

Interview with the exorcist Terry Stokes

In the course of researching this book I was privileged to interview one of the most experienced secular exorcists currently operating in the United Kingdom. His name is Mr Terry Stokes and this is a slightly edited and abridged account of the interview. I should make clear that Terry does not subscribe to any particular religious schism and uses whatever technique he deems necessary to conduct the rite.

"My early life was such that I had frequent exposure to psychic events and talked to invisible people. Children exposed to anything like psychic activity have no internal regulators and soak it up like a sponge, so I from a child, in fact especially as a child, was very psychic. As you get older you tend to rationalise stuff out, the internal regulator comes in and you say 'no' and many promising psychics are conditioned away from these natural impulses, and unfortunately the schooling system, especially the Roman Catholic ones that I attended, were absolutely horrified at the thought of a child with intuition."

"I found at primary school I would just know things about the other kids, and I could instinctively read hands, as my reputation increased I would be asked to pick out winners for dog and horse races, which probably only 50% was right, a friend took me to a spiritualist meeting when I was about 17, and I amazed them, I felt understood and appreciated at last and began training to be a medium, but some did not like this know nothing skinny, shy teenager coming from no where and taking the spotlight, and spiteful comments began and hateful things being said about my youth and where my information came from."

"Unhappy at all the attention I slipped into rescue circle work and then exorcism and found this my natural place, my style was very different then from later on. A family friend, Father Green, asked me what I thought about the real events behind the film 'The Exorcist', and he told me that the real events were too unpleasant to be shown on film and told me I was doing it all wrong and was surprised it worked at all. He said it was too magical and medieval for the 20th century, I saw him working and he encouraged me along new lines, which were more Catholic in nature. I was a quiet, withdrawn personality and did not relish being on a platform in front of scores of people, but was at home with spirits."

"The Rev Christopher Neil Smith made a great impression on me, people would come from all over the world, and so skilled was he that following his services he literally performed one exorcism after the other. I have no doubt many people were mentally ill, some physically too, but there were a percentage who bore every sign of demonic possession. The methods he used were similar, but more refined than my own and he was a great influence on me and my work. It was after a country house cleansing in 1971-2 that I met the noted Anglican exorcist Dom Robert Petit Pierre."

"Dom Robert was a quiet and holy man, who, at the time, was almost unknown and he told me about the noted Italian mystic and stigmatic Padre Pio, a man with such powers that he could cure the gravest ailments at a distance. Dom Robert was asked to exorcise the Queen Mother's house and no matter how many times I asked he would never discuss it, save that a child's soul was unhappy there. He also performed several exorcisms at the Astor's country estate where Christine Keeler and other beauties entertained the rich and famous", (see chapter 16),

"I had many successes such as the Dennis Nilsen * house and at the civil war battlefield at Naseby and my failures were not many, but one ceremony went badly wrong when I myself became possessed by an entity that caused me grave illness both mental and physical and this brought me back to earth with a bump. Initially I saw exorcism as a battle as that's how it was, fashions changed and it became 'deliverance' and in recent years I view what I have done as a healing and often did not evict a soul in anguish, but just healed and comforted it and left it to work out its own time to leave its physical surroundings."

"Although now I am quite well known as a teacher in spiritual studies, it should be said that my first introduction to spiritual matters was not a happy one. As a small child my family moved to a run down old shop in London, and like most little ones, I would see, hear and generally be aware of all sorts of spirit manifestation. This house had a pair of large iron hooks set inside the frame of what was then the kitchen doorway and having a fascination for them, as a child I would reach up and swing on these hooks, although it would be many years before I realised what they were originally used for. My father, like many others of his generation, came back from World War II a very damaged man, not physically but mentally and he appeared at times totally unable to think and feel, and would sit for hours in an arm-chair just staring at the wallpaper."

---

* Dennis Nilsen was a notorious, necrophiliac homosexual serial killer of fifteen men and boys who was imprisoned for life in 1983

"I can still remember him shouting in his sleep to "get your heads down boys" This exposure to suffering attracted all sorts of astral creatures, known as "*exuviae*" to his aura, and that of the house. I now realise he would never have got better in a house such as this. It has been established now that depression is one of the consequences of living in a haunted house, and the house had an empty, heavy and depressed feeling to it."

"Living in a haunted house can develop a child's psychic awareness at an early age and I still remember queuing for school dinners when I was seven years old, when a boy in front of me put up his hand in front of my eyes. As he did so events from his future began flashing before me, one superimposing on another, with all the intense emotion relevant to each one totally swamping my young mind and at the time, leaving me upset and confused. From that day, I have read hands for people the world over, always believing that the bottom line of any reading must be part of the healing process."

"The house itself was two hundred years old, and as I was to discover when I was in my twenties, the many alleyways around the property, which baffled me as a child were there to guide the animals to the house, which in days long past, had been an abattoir and butchers shop. You will be familiar with the fact that a shark can be attracted by spilt blood in the water from many miles away, so it is that some spirits in the air will be drawn to spilt blood and the killing of animals on a daily basis would attract some horrific astral entities."

"It has long been a method of black magicians to spill blood to bring the spirits, and some old religious cults still insist on cutting animals throats for the same reason. These Satanic rituals continue today with animal blood being smeared onto the faces of children in hunting re-enactments. While in Iraq the faces of detainees were "blooded" with the menstrual blood of prostitutes; this is a powerful weapon capable of psychologically programming the victims to attract demonic forces to the oldest part of the brain, the Hippocampus, via the breathing and autonomic nervous system."

"This can establish a deep connection with primordial forces that can grip a mind and destroy it; the torment and inner anguish produced resulting in a great desire to spill blood. The Native American Indian war paint produced a similar effect and was used when battle was felt inevitable. Even in the Roman Catholic rite of Holy Communion, prior to which a rite called the miracle of Transubstantiation is enacted, where the bread and wine is supposedly transformed by the magician or priest into the body and blood of Christ, is a more modern form of the same ritual. It is actually rather more that this and as far as the faithful are concerned God literally present on the altar."

"In wartime, spirit feeders on spilt blood will influence men to shed more blood, which attracts more primary demonic entities, who will influence men to shed even more. And it was these entities that would frighten me as a child at night, so much so that I was often barely able to move, or even breathe, in my bed at night. The sight and feel of some of these creatures will be with me always, and it is probably the close contact with these inhabitants of the lower realms that gave me the abilities of a healer and exorcist in later years."

"Animals respond in their own way to these forces. Take one to the vet and watch its reaction, it knows it is going to be slaughtered and its body produces the fear related chemical adrenaline. Just as a dog will smell fear on a human, so the blood imbibing creatures of the lower astral will smell the fear and adrenaline and feed on it. As a child I would regularly watch from my bed at night what I can only describe metaphorically throwing a lump of meat into the garden and a flock of cawing black crows will soon fly round squabbling over it, fighting for some of the life force in the meat."

"These lower realm creatures would flock and caw in the same way around and above my home. Necrophagia, or the eating of dead flesh, was said by the philosopher Empedocles to be the real original sin of the bible. There has always been argument and controversy over whether it is right to kill an animal to eat its meat, and I have studied this issue for many years, but please understand that where blood is spilt the lower spirits will gather and like the house I lived in as a child, it will not be a pleasant place and this aura will persist for many years."

"When playing in the garden as a child I would dig up lots of bones and, as children do, thought I might have found a dinosaur, and the metal hooks in the doorway from which I would swing was where the animals were hung upside down for the separation of their limbs. This only became apparent to me after many years. Houses such as this are emotional sink-pits where no happiness or kindness exists, any encouraging words are immediately dissolved in the air, no romantic prosperity, contentment or warmth can exist here, and the human inhabitants of such premises also embody some aspect of the walking wounded."

"Unhappiness does not exist in a vacuum however. It is contagious and I've often found that when called to exorcise buildings, the people living there often need either exorcism or spiritual healing themselves. A certain denial can accompany these people who often exhibit symptoms of either emotional numbness, or persistent sarcasm, even sexual promiscuity or some other toxic character deficiency, which prevents integration with others and successful relationships."

Chapter 16
Exorcism and What Can go Wrong

interviewed Terry again a few weeks later regarding his feelings about exorcism and what follows is his account of what can occur at an exorcism, because unfortunately they do not always go to plan.

"This is a disaster story from start to finish, which ended my spiritual career. Some six years ago I had a frantic call from a young woman who had come to me not from one of the spiritual organisations I serve, but from an old colleague in psychology and comparative religious studies."

"I rushed into the whole thing; I have often wanted to invent "retrospectacles" whereby the wisdom of retrospect would be available from the start. In retrospect we usually all have 20/20 vision and looking back I should not have been so distressed when a woman arrived at my door after a frantic phone call on Halloween day. She was a hospital worker with a name badge bearing the name "Helene". She told me she was an illegal worker from Nigeria whose real name was Shanni."

"This is not unusual, a recent well publicised case of shoplifting revealed a Londoner who was a refugee with 128 different identities and passports and the recent explosion of different cultures and nationalities has made it difficult for us to keep abreast of the misuse of religious rituals and psychic powers here in Britain. This lady began pouring out in my little front room a textbook case of "Kendocki witchcraft". *Note, Kendocki is a traditional African variety of magick and spell casting.*

"Due to the debased African Evangelical witchcraft rites now becoming common in Britain's major cities, the sense of urgency was very real, to act fast. 'Bushmeat' comprises animal and human carcase parts. I had acted as an adviser to Scotland Yard in these matters and watched as a black candidate, John Sentamu, was chosen as Archbishop of York recently, hoping he would speak out to stop the advance of this abominable trade."

"This bushmeat is for primitive medicines, black magick and human consumption and is in greater demand in Britain's multiracial inner cites than ever before. In Voodoo ceremonies the Houngan (or magician/high priest) hypnotises the person before slaying them, to the effect that, when dead, the spirit will do his bidding in the twilight world between this world and the next, in much the same way that the ancient Egyptians would protect corpses and buildings."

"This is the true biblical meaning of necromancy or a "Keeper of spirits". To clarify a little, the Houngan, although acting as a high priest in the Voodoo religion, has a female counterpart known as the 'mambo'. There are also lesser, but still powerful priests, a cast of workers known as 'bocors' who are ordained by individual Houngons. This is not, as some sectarians say, the way in which spiritualists prepare and sensitise themselves to communicate and this is an important difference."

"The young woman told me she was one of this magicians slaves and she sent him money and from time to time she would be compelled either by telephone or telepathy to go to him. This beautiful, intelligent woman with her hourglass figure said as long as she would periodically slake his physical appetite she would be safe from the wrath of the Ngozi."

"Part of an exorcists training is in first seeing and particularly feeling into other realms by many months of eye exercises and concentrated auric strengthening, meditation, concentration and diet. Then developing those aspects of a healer that would be used in separating the magician from the victim, largely by means of astral psuedopods. I could sense the magician as a big black spider in the centre of its web, with maybe six other victims magnetically caught in the force."

"We both knew that any movement from Shanni or myself, emotional, physical or spiritual, would cause the web to tremble bringing death to her, from her keeper or from the unseen hands of one of the hypnotised Ngozi or "undead". This poor girl said she would risk death to be free and recklessly I said this was achievable. I had come up against several magicians, spirit manipulators and controllers in the past and even when out-skilled and outclassed had always won and gave her strict instructions of what to do and how to sleep that night."

"But in the Hypnagogic and Hypnapompic stages between sleep and wakefulness, in my blessed and psychically fortified bedroom, there appeared a large cobra snake poised to strike in a sudden attack of such ferocity. I have fought these and other serpents off before, but it was so quick and bit me before I got away." "The next few days saw my health and strength dissipating and when Shanni visited she told me she could not come again as I could not help, and the magician told her I was to die. This was a last warning to her, and matters were not helped as she went away in abject despair when I saw the magicians mark of a cobra tattooed on her arm, these magicians always mark or brand their goods and she was his property."

"Over the next few months I would many times collapse on the floor unable to breathe, with trembling and sickness. My manager at work harassed and bullied me to leave my job. I was variously diagnosed as having asbestosis of the lung, C.O.P.D (Chronic obstructive pulmonary disorder) and something called 'Weggoners Granulomatosis', all with a life expectancy of around a year." "Specialists at the hospital could not agree on my malady and whatever medication they tried did not work. My G.P gave me the drug 'Serevent', said by the American F.D.A to be implicated in of 90% of all respiratory deaths. I have had numerous near death experiences, in one case being revived in a hospital casualty department, the staff there suspected brain damage as I had been out so long. Five years on and I cannot move far from a home machine that takes over my breathing for periods in the day, and most of the night, I can only walk a few steps and my expectancy of life is short."

"But the worst part was when the newspapers contained the story of a young African nurse who, while disturbed, took a drug overdose and committed suicide by jumping from her window. I was summoned to a committee meeting at the "Interspiritual Forum" for a *'Lucobration'*. This is a learned spiritual discourse or interrogation on my methods of spirit assistance, risk assessment, counselling exorcism and healing prognosis and they told me to bring all my awards and certifications and asked me to explain how, when in my care, this tragedy could happen."

"I stood before the committee and had questions barked at me and it was humiliatingly adduced during the break that I was deemed to be negligent. I was asked to resign and to pass back my awards from my five years as the forum's top healer and exorcist. As I stood before the panel in shame my certificates were torn up in front of me, and the decagonal ten year service cup silver cup returned." "The committee asked me several times why I did not come and ask its help? Why there was so little background information on my written notes, and if I was out of my depth, and I did not believe I was, how could I let this happen? Why did I not ask for an emergency meeting at any time to find the *"Libken"*, which is the vulnerable sleeping lair of the beast or magician, for an all out spiritual assault? But I did not."

"In law any healer has what is called a "duty of care" and for whatever reason this young nurse died on my watch. Suddenly you are no longer invited to lecture or speak, my Christmas cards dropped by more than half, whispers were that I was over the hill, had lost it and was finished. Even my phone did not ring. I compared this with hospital doctors and General Practitioners whose mistakes kill people every day and all the time protected by the B.M.A (British Medical Association) and thought that I had tumbled from the absolute top to the very bottom."

"We in Britain could not understand why America treated President Nixon so badly when all politicians do the same, I remembered his words; *"he who has not stood at the bottom of the valley, cannot appreciate the view from the mountain top"*, I am patiently waiting to again see the view from my mountain top. With retrospect maybe the verdict of the inter-spiritual forum is right and I was negligent,

but I fully believe with the wisdom of retrospect that even today I would take
exactly the same protective measures."

That ended my second interview with Terry and it was truly fascinating to learn
that such practises are still a part of life in the modern world; truly the old ways
die hard, or perhaps they are still quite valid, but simply sidelined and ignored in
the secular society in which we live.

Chapter 17
Exorcism
Psychological, Psycho-Sexual or Paranormal?

What follows is the product of a third and final interview with Terry, which gives another account of exorcism in London.

"There is much argument in the spiritual press right now among scholars as to what an exorcism really is. Should it be a psychological process? Is it a spiritual or psychiatric sickness? Can depressive treatments help? My old colleague, the Rev David Tyndall, was featured in the newspapers recently. David, whom I admire greatly for his expertise, has for some years been a well known Christian cleric and he confided in me that although he is a bible scholar, a talented psychologist and grief counsellor, he had attended over thirty-three exorcisms in his seventeen years in the church. In that time had never seen anything which definitely convinced him of the existence of the paranormal. Where you draw the guidelines in these issues is crucial and for a man of religion to say he did not believe in the supernatural, when the religious word 'miracle' means white magick, and the sacraments are themselves a magical rite, is strange indeed.?"

"The Rev. Christopher Neil-Smith (unfortunately now deceased is rumoured by 'inside sources' to have helped John Lennon, just prior to, and maybe during, his involvement with Yoko Ono and before his assassination, when he was under close F.B.I surveillance. Rev. Neil-Smith saw evidence of the paranormal everywhere he looked, those who watched him work were amazed at the speed of his skills, people came from all over the world to see him and he taught us so much. The Rev Neil–Smith is reckoned to have conducted over three thousand exorcisms since 1949 in Britain alone and in 1973 the Bishop of London gave him permission to conduct exorcism using his own judgement. "

"Certainly in my prime I was on call for anywhere in the country and for many years could often do one a week, and in all fairness the amount of times I saw real phenomena was very rare, yet whenever I am interviewed for the media, it is these instances that I have to keep recounting. I reminded David Tyndall of the Bishop Felton (pseudonym) case, now although this has never reached the public domain, I know of several of the people involved and can vouch for its authenticity."

"As I remember it, in 1970 a late night phone call was made by a group of youngsters, who, after a party at a tower block in London's Stratford area, contacted the Catholic Church to say that the group had brought up an intelligence from a game on an Ouija board and that this 'intelligence' had occupied one of these youngsters who was now showing extreme paranormal abilities. This sort of story is part of the chaff that is interspersed with the precious wheat of knowledge, and in the ordinary way I confess would take little notice of, but coming from David Tyndall, Fr. Kenneth Green and Bishop Felton himself, I had to listen and take notice."

"Before an exorcism can take place permission from the Diocesan Bishop must be granted and the area exorcist, a man chosen usually for his knowledge or holiness brought in. So serious did the Bishop consider the apparent danger to the youngsters involved to be that he immediately went to the scene while phoning two experts to meet him at the tower block. So all three, the Bishop and the two priests, all experts in their field remember, met up at the flat to give assistance. Over the years we all have perhaps met people who have benefited from their research with Ouija boards and stories of all kinds are told about it. My own opinion is that most of the information is from the unconscious minds of the sitters, but alas horror stories are also very common."

"The Bishop, who was an outspoken and fearless man in what he believed, had become well known when he protested at the torture of German detainees at the Nuremberg war crimes trials. He had also objected to the Catholic Church giving last rites and Catholic funerals to I R A killers and bombers because it is actually canon dogma (the rigid set of rules that govern how the church functions) that no one who has committed a 'mortal sin' such as murder can be buried in consecrated ground. However the Church is quite capable of turning a blind eye when it wants to, as the recent spate of sex scandals that caused so much ill feeling clearly demonstrates."

"The Bishop's story, which was told in the greatest detail by the two priests, suggests that when he entered the room in the tower block, the possessed youngster spoke to him in a deep, metallic, gravely voice and mocked him by saying that he was not a good enough man to exorcise him. The voice claimed that he had slept with a woman some five years before, and liked a secret night time drop of Scots whisky. The sheer strength of the youngster made it necessary for the three churchmen to hold him while the deliverance was attempted and at times all three were simultaneously lifted off the ground. Objects seemed to just fly round the room, and the Bishop seized the youth by the lapels and began screaming through the insane laughter the Catholic exorcism rites, I was told that the Bishop struggled with the beast inside the youth into the small hours of the morning before they could all safely leave the tower block."

"So, to answer the esteemed David Tyndall, I am sure that most times the causes are just psychological, other causes can be paranormal or even emotio/physical. However, I would stress the following to all who would wish to push the boundaries of this knowledge. As the master occultist Rollo Ahmed, one of Dennis Wheatley's top pupils once said; *"The dangers in the unseen worlds are very real indeed, and never, ever to be trifled with.* Good advice for the curious, so how safe are readings?"

Chapter 19
Sex, Death and Exorcism

I t is indeed strange that, in terms of what this book is about, those who have the most, in material terms at least, also appear to be afflicted with a terminal ennui that runs a terrifyingly close parallel to an instinct for self-destruction. And so it was in the born again freedom of the 1960s, when the rich and powerful came out to play and became mired in a web of promiscuous sex, scandal, alcohol, the use of illicit drugs and, perhaps inevitably the ultimate thrill...black magick!

It was this last unhealthy option that, as we shall see, led to at least one case of apparent possession. It was also an era when pretty much anything went and it was also a time, in the United Kingdom at least, when the traditional values represented by church and state were seen as a hindrance and irrelevance. However, as we shall see in one particular set of circumstances, the services of an officer of the Church were required to undo some of the damage that had been done.

In many ways the values of the 1960s were a juddering hammer blow to the lynchpins of the rigid, class-ridden and elitist cohorts of the UK when, as a direct result of the social and cultural changes created by the Second World War, much had changed, and from their perspective the world would never be the same again. This new era of 'flower power' and liberal empowerment, not to mention the explosion in the recreational use of drugs, irrevocably and permanently changed the social landscape. To a great extent the 'old order' had also changed, and the hidebound elite whose indiscretions enjoyed automatic censorship and concealment now found themselves exposed to the glare of egalitarian openness.

It might not have mattered too much had those who chose this risky (and frequently risqué) lifestyle only been the bored and/or idle rich. In that context they might have enjoyed their brief flare of fame (or notoriety) and been exposed by the sensation seeking gutter press as rich wastrels who were good for column inches and little else. However, the lifestyle also attracted those who would have been better served by avoiding the siren song of excess. Every circus needs a ringmaster, for indeed a circus it was, and in this case the master, in more ways than one, was an influential and talented society osteopath and sometime portrait artist, the late Dr Stephen Ward. However, before we look behind the veil of obfuscation and misdirection still surrounding the wild drug and alcohol-fuelled sex parties he organised for the powerbrokers, politicians and their associates, we should look at the man.

Stephen Ward was born in 1912 into a traditional Anglican family; and his father, Arthur Ward, was the Canon of Rochester Cathedral. Stephen was initially educated at Highgate School in London, but a few years later, in 1920, the family moved to Torquay when Arthur Ward was appointed Vicar at the church of St Matthias. Stephen's early life was relatively uneventful until, aged seventeen, his family wanted him to attend university, but he refused and moved first to London then Hamburg, where, in 1929, he found employment as a translator at the German branch of the oil giant Shell. In 1934, Ward's mother convinced him that his future lay elsewhere and he travelled to America to study osteopathy at the Kirksville Collage in Missouri. During this time he developed a deep and abiding love of America and the warmth and friendliness of its people, which was a sharp contrast to the 'stiff upper lip' iciness that typified much of English society.

After the Second World War, when he served with the Royal Armoured Corps, Ward worked for the Osteopathic Association Clinic in Dorset Square in London. It was here that he met and treated several extremely influential and powerful people including the iconic wartime prime minister, Winston Churchill, cabinet minister Duncan Sandys, (the Minister for Aviation), the artist Feliks Topolski and film stars Ava Gardiner, Mary Martin (mother of 'Dallas' actor Larry Hagman) and Mel Ferrer. His exclusive clientele slowly built up, allowing him to open his own clinic at Cavendish Square in the immediate vicinity of the epicentre of expensive private medicine in fashionable Harley Street. It is interesting that given the nature of what Ward later became involved in, that Duncan Sandys was also embroiled in a notorious sexual escapade involving the Duchess of Argyle and the actor Douglas Fairbanks Jr.

Among those he also befriended were Lord Astor, who allowed him free use of a cottage on his sprawling Cliveden Estate, and also Sir Roger Hollis, at that time the head of MI5. He also socialised with such people as the art historian and soviet spy Anthony Blunt, the aforementioned actor Douglas Fairbanks Jr, Prince Philip, the Marquis of Milford and the notorious slum landlord Peter Rachman. It was these associations, coupled to his need to ingratiate himself further, that almost by osmosis lead to him to become what was in effect a pimp supplying attractive young women such as Christine Keeler and Mandy Rice-Davies (to whom Ward at one point proposed marriage) for the many extravagant parties he hosted at the cottage on Lord Astor's estate. It was during this period that he met the individuals who were to play such an important part in the scandal that brought down a government, and led to his death, supposedly through suicide.

The parties/orgies were one thing, but it was his association with the communist sympathiser Anthony Blunt and latterly Yevgeni Ivanov, the Soviet Naval Attaché that ultimately destroyed the reputation and career of John Profumo, the anachronistically named 'Minister for War' in the Conservative government. The act that finally brought down Profumo was his sworn declaration to parliament that he had not had an affair with the call girl Christine Keeler. The truth, or otherwise, of the situation is, quite typically in situations like this, fluid. Profumo was indeed having an affair with Keeler and that is known, but probably unaware that she was also sleeping with Ivanov.

The fear, as far as the British government was concerned, was due to what is euphemistically known as 'pillow talk', when state secrets might find their way to the Soviet Union. Bad enough you might think, but it is strongly implied that Stephen Ward was in fact an MI5 asset and attempting to entrap Ivanov using the classic 'honey pot' ruse. In fact the entire affair was part and parcel of a convoluted spy network involving the so called 'Cambridge Five', which included the Surveyor of the Queen's Pictures (the then Sir) Anthony Blunt, plus Kim Philby, Guy Burgess, John Caircross and Donald Mclean, all of whom were under intense scrutiny from the security services.

Even this group may not have been the final summation, because the English university system was a fertile recruiting ground for Soviet talent spotters like Arnold Deuch and there may well have been other spies deliberately allowed to remain at large to suit the Machiavellian plans of the British security services. An interesting observation made about British security is that the end always justifies the means, and that was made by a member of the Russian security services; a back-handed compliment if ever there was one.

The network of spies at this time was an international spider's web of intrigue reaching into all the powerbases of the military and government in the UK and all of them had been 'turned' by charismatic and urbane individuals like Anthony Blunt, who escaped prosecution by informing on his former associates. Even then there are suspicions that some of them were in fact double, and even treble, agents operated (or 'run' as the saying goes) by the Soviet Union, the United States and of course the United Kingdom. Bear in mind that all this was happening during the heightened suspicion and paranoia surrounding the 'Cold War' when nuclear war between the superpowers was a very real risk and spying was rife.

In any event, as part of the fallout from the whole sorry affair, Ward was arrested under the Sexual Offences Act 1956 on charges of living off immoral earnings, and Christine Keeler was arrested for prostitution. At this point MI5 denied all knowledge of Ward and insisted that he never told them about Profumo's involvement with Christine Keeler and by implication Yevgeni Ivanov. During the 1963 trial, following a severe character assassination at the hands of the prosecution counsel, Mervin Griffin-Jones, Ward overdosed on barbiturates and was found in a coma from which he never awoke and died a few weeks later.

The trial was concluded on the 5th of August 1963 with no sentence passed. Did Ward jump or was he pushed? The answer to this is unknown, but there is little doubt that he was privy to some juicy and highly embarrassing titbits of information and he may well have been assassinated 'just in case'. Well, this tidies away all the aspects of the affair that were fit to be seen, but it did not of course reveal all that had occurred, nor those involved; *especially* those who had been involved.

Another aspect of what came to be known as 'The Profumo Affair' that was also overlooked, almost certainly deliberately, was the fact that in addition to being an osteopath and gifted artist, Ward was also a practising magician. The 'poolside parties' he organised at the cottage on the Cliveden Estate of Lord Astor, although undoubtedly louche, extravagant and lascivious affairs, were window-dressing for the other, much, much, darker 'games'. This information did not emerge until after the death of Ward when he could no longer be called upon to testify, although, that said, not all of those present at the parties would have been privy to the excesses of the magickal rituals invoked by Ward; they were only for a privileged few initiates seeking more intense thrills.

It is doubtful that even among this 'elite' there were very few who, at the outset at least, would have been aware of the risks involved. While the actual use of sorcery by Ward and his inner circle had no apparent practical purpose other than to provide an extra level of excitement and channel for boredom, it now seems that there was much more to it than that. However, before we return to that, the involvement of the security services with magick goes back for some considerable way, right back to the Elizabethan magus, Dr John Dee in fact.

John Dee was a truly remarkable man. He was an alchemist, a mathematician, an astrologer and of course a magician, a real polymath and he also created (or transcribed depending on how one views it) the Enochian alphabet. This strange selection of enigmatic glyphs and shapes was apparently given to him, by the 'angels' he observed using magickal techniques, and a bizarre scrying device made of obsidian (volcanic glass). He is also known to have been deeply involved with Sir Francis Walsingham who founded the first effective English Secret Service during the reign of Queen Elizabeth I, and it has been mooted that Dee's 'Enochian' symbols were in fact used as form of code to convey secret messages.

Curiously enough the code number assigned to Dr Dee was 007, the same as Ian Fleming's creation James Bond, and of course Fleming was also involved to some extent with magick through the medium Helen Duncan, and - of course - the almost ubiquitous and notorious magician Aleister Crowley. The use of the Enochian language has become part and parcel of various types of magick and is frequently used in the rituals involved.

Another character involved with both the security services and magick was Sir Francis Dashwood, founder of the 'Hellfire Club', which had much in common with the more lurid excesses of Stephen Ward and his associates. The security interest was more due to the importance of the attendees at the Hellfire Club than anything else. Dashwood attracted some degree of infamy in another context too when he undertook the 'Grand Tour' of Europe, something that at the time was practically *de rigueur* for young men of his wealth and status.

After joining the Masonic Order in France he then went to Italy where he developed markedly anti-Catholic views. These were formed when he observed the stark differences between the wealth of casual ostentation of the Church and the crushing poverty of the majority of their devout flock. This found expression when he disrupted a Mass and openly insulted the Pope, however in the long term it did him no harm and he eventually was elected to the British Government and became Chancellor of the Exchequer.

We have briefly mentioned Aleister Crowley; a man who has become almost ubiquitous as far as magick is concerned. Despite his largely deserved notoriety, Crowley always claimed that he worked for, or at least cooperated with, British Intelligence during both the First and Second World Wars. It is also strongly hinted that he was directly involved in the interrogation of Rudolph Hess and was brought in specifically to do this by a young intelligence officer named Ian Fleming, who went on to become the creator of James Bond. Fleming, who knew him, and in particular his encyclopaedic practical knowledge of the occult.

Fleming was himself at least peripherally involved in another aspect of magick when he was instrumental in the arrest of the Scottish medium Helen Duncan who, during a séance, revealed that the *HMS Barham* had been sunk with a considerable loss of life when this was still a closely guarded secret. The propaganda and news management during wartime was almost a form of magick in its own right, a primitive type of thought control.

The most recent collaboration between the security services and magick must surely be the events surrounding the so-called 'Stargate Project' when certain carefully selected people were trained to 'remote view' objects and individuals thousands of miles away. It has been rumoured that the remote viewers were able, in some situations, to travel off planet and even travel in time. However, the source of funding for the project ceased in 1995, although it has been reported that three of the best remote viewers were seconded onto another, as yet unnamed, project. The original idea came from a genuine fear that the Russians had begun a similar project as far back as 1977 when US Army Intelligence (INSCOM) instituted the forerunner to Stargate and called it 'Gondola Wish'.

If we can accept, even hypothetically, that the intelligence services can and do forms of magick, they must therefore consider it viable, so - if Ward and his initiates were not simply looking for enhanced sexual thrills - what were they doing? In some cases sexual excess is essential to rituals that involve Tantric practises such as those used by the Ordo Templi Orientis (OTO), therefore what Ward was doing was legitimate, but again why?

Was it because some of his coven were in important positions and wanted to guarantee that they would remain so, was it because of power or influence or was it simply money? It has been alleged that magick and those who practise it are interested in attaining a combination of sex, power and money, and sometimes all three. What is clear is that Ward was involved in magickal practises that were extremely dangerous. If so then these rituals can and do leave an unhealthy residue, a sort of 'psychic stench' in and around the area they are practised, and so it was with the cottage on the Cliveden Estate.

Following the demise of Ward and the break up of his circle of friends, the cottage was used and lived in by various people, but now there was a permanent uneasy and unhealthy ambience attached to it. There were reports of 'bumps in the night', and also frequent glimpses of terrifying apparitions, but more worryingly there were full-blown manifestations of poltergeist phenomena. These continued for some time and were either ignored or at best tolerated, until during one period of occupation one of the guests displayed what can best be described as classic and dramatic symptoms of demonic possession.

This resulted in arrangements being made to have the place exorcised and the man chosen to perform this rite was the noted Anglican exorcist, the late Dom Robert Petit-Pierre. According to Dom Robert, the place took a full two days of concentrated effort to expunge it of whatever had taken hold of the building. The exorcist was certain that Ward had indulged in black magick and Satanism and the exorcism was one of the most complex he had ever undertaken. Evidently it was a success and there were no further reports of disturbances there. The person whose possession had caused the cleansing to take place apparently recovered after some suitable therapy, but unfortunately the nature of the therapy is not clear.

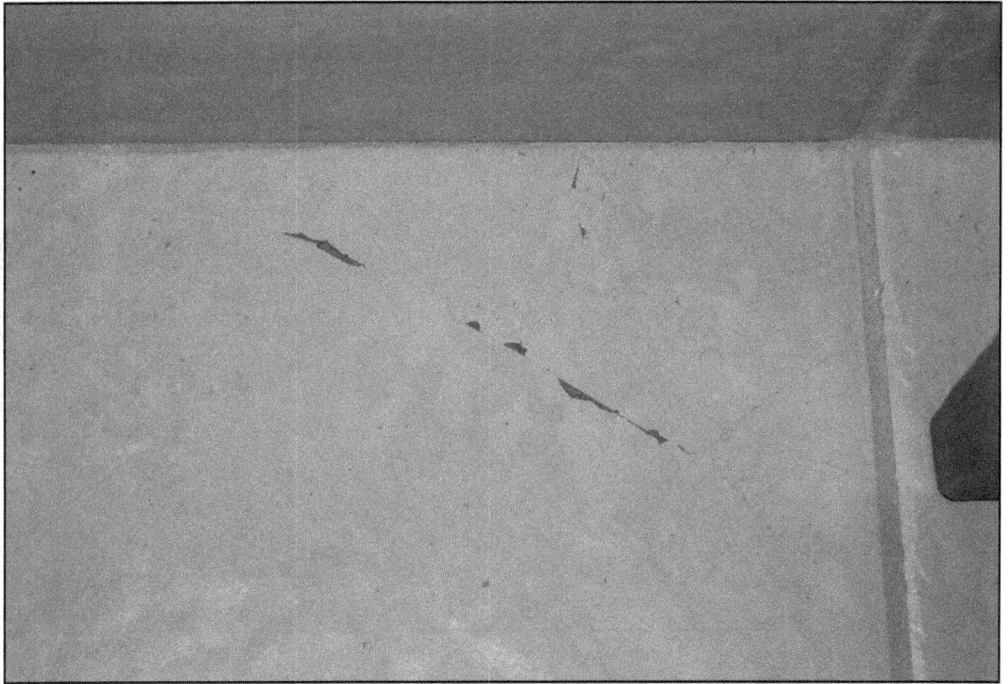

ABOVE: Chapter 21 - 33 'A Remote Exorcism'.
Damage caused by entity to interior of house
BELOW: Ch 21 - 33 'A Remote Exorcism'.
More damage to house interior this time showing the twin track marks

ABOVE: chapters 21 - 33 'A Remote Exorcism'. Damage to interior of house
BELOW: Chapter 34 'Scratches'. Injuries to Andy's arm

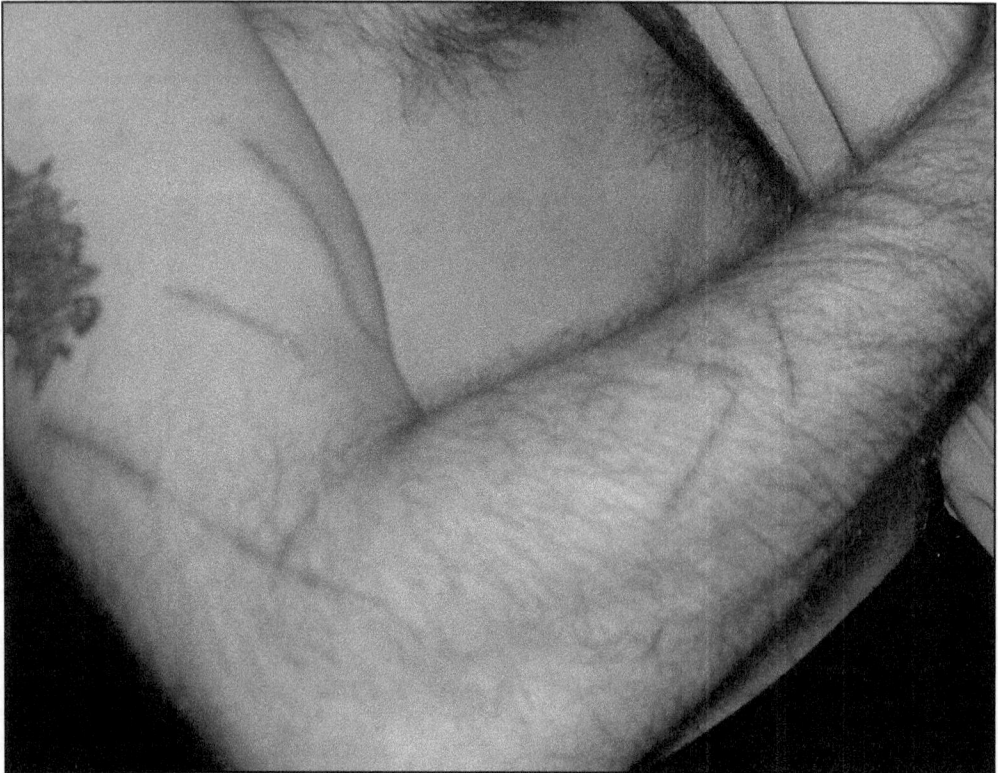

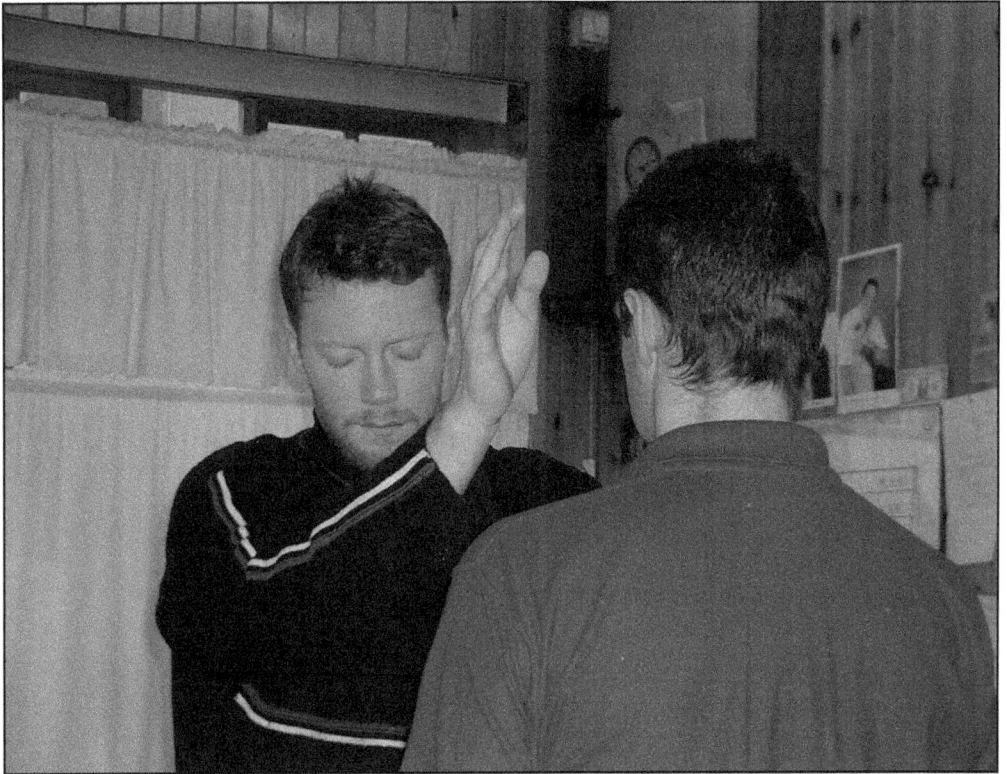

ABOVE: Chapter 34, 'Scratches'. 'John' conducting exorcism on Andy
BELOW: Ch 21-33 'A Remote Exorcism'. More interior damage to house

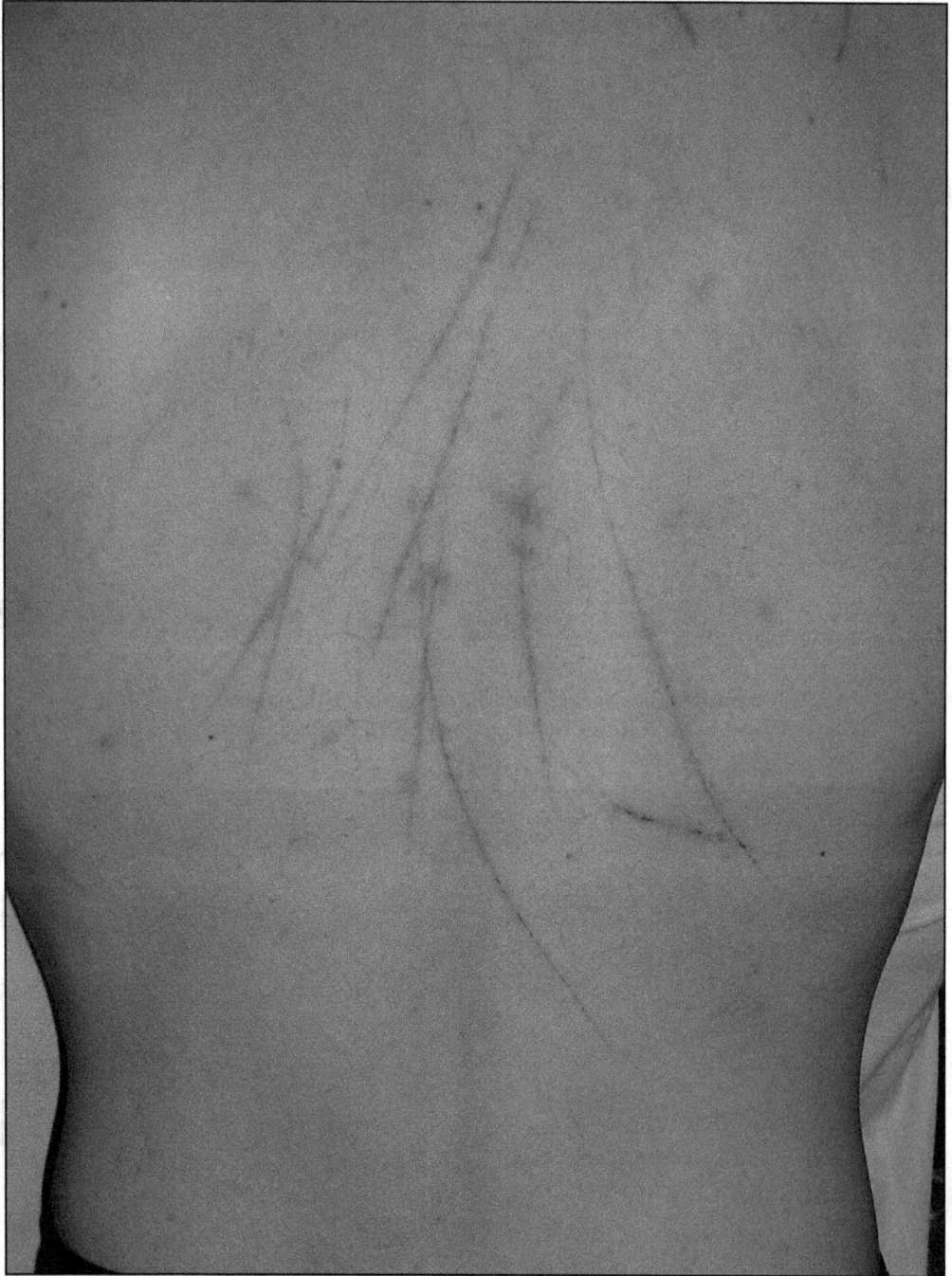

Chapter 34 'Scratches'. Injuries inflicted on Andy's back

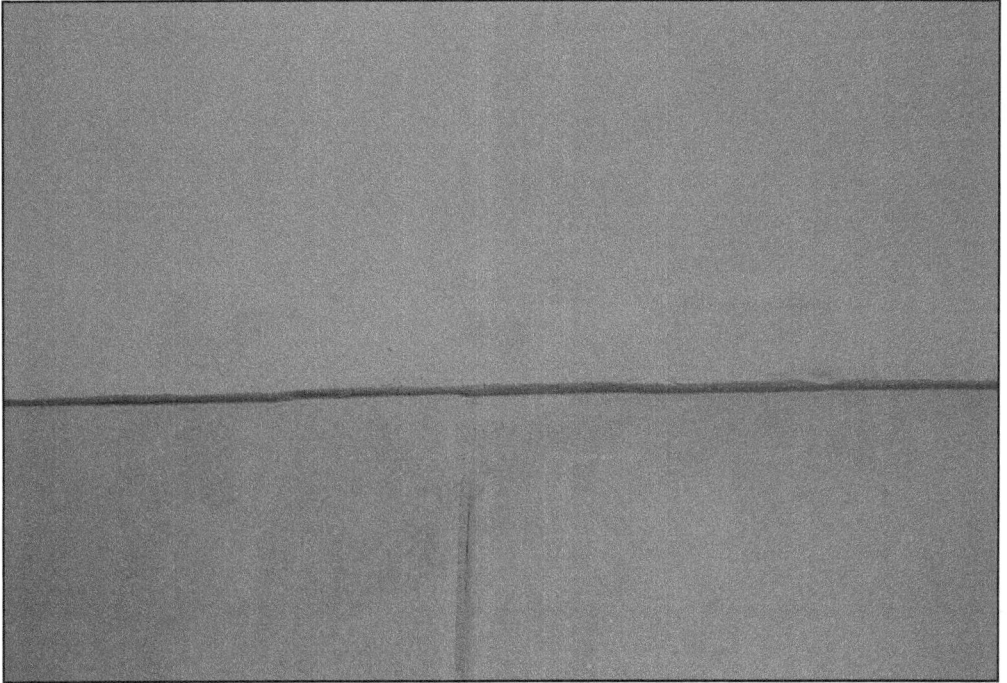

ABOVE: Ch 21 - 33 'A Remote Exorcism'.
Showing mysterious colour change caused by entity
BELOW: Ch 21 - 33 'A Remote Exorcism'. Damage to grout plus colour changes

ABOVE: Ch 21 - 33 'A Remote Exorcism'.
Damage to work top edges all caused by invading entity
BELOW: Ch 21 - 33 'A Remote Exorcism'.
Damage caused by entity to picture frame

Ch 21 - 33 ' A Remote Exorcism' Damage to stones outside house,
again cased by entity

Chapter 20
Vampire Hunters and Collectors

Tales of exorcists and miracle workers have now become so embedded in our culture, especially in recent times, that it can be difficult to separate fact from fantasy. There is no doubt that the supposedly demonic entities such as vampires and their fearless exorcising foes have evolved into something considerably more than an enigmatic shape changer with demonic associations. Instead, these often-terrifying, blood-drinking immortals and their nemeses have become the very epitome of stylish sophistication and cool.

The sybaritic lifestyle of the vampire has become a byword for all that is romantic, sensuous and hedonistic. The only downside to this is that in order to achieve such a nirvanic state one has, unfortunately, to be dead...or undead to be absolutely correct, and from all accounts the transformation process is not exactly pleasant. All of this is in direct opposition to the image of that other iconic shape-changer and traditional foe of the vampire: the werewolf; but that is another legend entirely, which has its roots in shamanism.

Although shape-changers have millennia-long histories in folklore, especially in shamanic traditions, the modern image of the vampire first appeared in the early 19th Century from a short story written by Dr John Polidori entitled *The Vampyre*. The tale centred round a supernatural aristocratic fiend who, in order to survive, consumed the blood of his peers. This struck a resonant chord in the psyche of the general public and morphed into other similar creatures starting with Bram Stoker's long-lived, much imitated, but never equalled, Dracula and also into generic offshoots like Count Orlok in another classic of the oeuvre, Nosferatu.

However the only one that actually stayed the course and fired the imagination was the aristocratic (and as a rule also autocratic) Count Dracula. Quite why this should be, especially now, is not too difficult to work out. Perhaps it has a lot to do with a desire to emulate the lifestyles of the rich and famous with the additional bonus of black magick, plus a smidgeon of sex, immortality and general naughtiness thrown in. A version of all this can be see in two separate, but thematically connected film (and book) franchises, i.e. the *Twilight* series and of course *Underworld*. While both of the variant tales effectively highlight the differences between vampires and werewolves, *Underworld* is by far the more effective, gritty and visceral. That said, one (*Twilight*) is designed to appeal to mainly female teenage audiences, while the other is not.

For all that, and in spite of the obvious links to fiction, this has not prevented a thin layer of belief that such creatures really do exist to take root, and not only in places like Transylvania and Romania, both traditional homes of the vampires. In the case of the undead, unholy creatures of the night mentioned here, each had their nemesis in the form of vampire hunters intent on destroying them, charismatic individuals like Abraham van Helsing, and, appropriately, even fictional characters like that found an analogue in the real world.

The belief in the reality of vampires and vampire-like creatures even reached the shores of the United Kingdom and this was almost a century after Stoker's fictional Dracula set foot on these shores at Whitby in the north of England. A more concrete and recent example of a belief in the reality of vampires first emerged in the 1960s when a group of people in London, all amateur ghosthunters, began conducting their dubious research in the marvellously atmospheric Highgate Cemetery in London.

It has to be said that this decaying and overgrown urban city of the dead has all the necessary credentials to be a ready made film set for horror films. In 1969 one of this investigative group, David Farrant, wrote an account of spending a night there and according to him, he had caught a glimpse of a supernatural grey figure (but, significantly, not a vampire) and the word soon spread. Shortly after this event, several other witnesses came forward with similar tales of ghostly figures drifting around the graveyard: and this is when, as they say, the plot thickens.

Sean Manchester

Following Farrant's announcement a second seeker appeared on the scene, a local man called The Rev. Sean Manchester, who was determined to track down and eliminate this ghostly presence. According to Manchester this was no ordinary spectre, but was instead a Vampire King of the Undead. Manchester said that this entity was a medieval, black magick-practising minor member of the Romanian nobility, who had been brought into this country in a coffin by some followers during the 1700s.

He had been buried in the area that had since become Highgate Cemetery. Manchester was adamant that the activities of modern Satanists had roused this creature and the only course of action was to locate the body, drive a wooden stake through its heart, behead it and burn the body. This was splendid, lip-smacking, meaty stuff and sensing a bit of sensation, local and national newspapers went into overdrive. A short time later both men stated that they had seen the remains of several foxes in the cemetery, all with their throats torn out, and completely drained of blood.

Farrant and Manchester had by now declared a sort of 'bidding war', with each of them trying to outdo the other with claims of how they intended to permanently remove the perceived menace. Manchester, a former president of the British Occult Society, eventually announced that he would conduct an exorcism on Friday the 13th of March 1970 and in the early evening of that date the location was inundated with a horde of curious thrill seekers. What occurred next is not 100% clear, nor is it fully independently verifiable. What evidence there is comes from Manchester's own account set out in his book of the affair, *The Highgate Vampire*, which he wrote in 1991, and this glowing and rather breathless account of what went on can be condensed as follows.

To avoid a police cordon that had been placed around the main cemetery to thwart the crowds that had assembled, Manchester and some associates entered the cemetery covertly via an adjoining graveyard. Once inside and using the talents of a female psychic they located a vault that, the medium said, was the vampire's lair. They repeatedly attempted to force the heavy vault door (which was made of iron) open, but were unable so to do. Not to be thwarted, they then climbed up on the roof of the tomb and gained entry via ropes lowered through a hole, and once inside found several empty coffins. Assuming that the occupants of the coffins were currently otherwise engaged in gruesome pursuits, using one of the traditional anti-vampire techniques they placed cloves of garlic in the coffins finishing up with a generous sprinkle of holy water. After this they climbed back up the ropes (they must have been very well prepared, not to mention fit) and surreptitiously left the cemetery through the point of entry.

Whether their efforts were fruitful is not clear, but a few months later the charred remains of a female corpse were discovered a short distance from the vault. It is assumed this was the handiwork of the Satanic groups that, to this day, still use the location for their ceremonies. It was also at around this time that Manchester's main competition (and another notorious self-publicist,) David Farrant, was discovered in the cemetery brandishing a crucifix and wooden stake; he was duly arrested, but when he appeared in court no charges were pressed.

Farrant persevered in his attempts at vampire hunting in Highgate Cemetery and was eventually jailed for desecrating graves and interfering with the dead. The means of dissuading individuals from disinterring remains is dealt with slightly differently in Scotland where there is something called the 'Right of Sepulchre' which specifically forbids it. This legal proscription has been used in places of considerable historic and occult interest, like Rosslyn Chapel, to prevent legitimate archaeological investigations taking place.

Eventually the increasing and intense rivalry between these two men culminated in rumours of an eagerly anticipated 'magicians duel' that was supposed to take place on Parliament Hill, but to much dismay it did not materialise. This so called 'magicians duel' must call into questions the motivations and outlook of both men. Such a duel (similar to one that really did take place between the previously mentioned iconic ritual magician Aleister Crowley and the one time head of the Golden Dawn, Samuel Liddell MacGregor Mathers) strongly implies that both men had deep knowledge of the subject. Given their relative youth it is unlikely that either of them had sufficient knowledge of this highly dangerous art to engage in such a battle, so it is more likely that this announcement was more to do with attention seeking, and grossly inflated egos than anything else.

Before leaving the actions of Sean Manchester we should perhaps look a little more closely at the man. Manchester, who in addition to his claims about the reality of vampires also holds the rank of Bishop and Primate of the *Ecclesia Apostolica Jesu Christi,* or *The Apostolic Church of Jesus Christ in Great Britain.* This church, whose first bishop was apparently Christ's uncle, Joseph of Arimathea, claims to have been consecrated by none other than Jesus Christ himself and arrived in Britain around AD 36. However, the church is also (and better) known by the name of *'The Old Catholic Church',* and is an offshoot of the traditional Roman Catholic Church as we know it today. It does however have a powerful connection with another vampire hunter and (among other things) self-styled exorcist, the late (and some might say notorious) Montague Summers. While examining the record of Summers, the reader will learn quite a lot about the ethos of Old Catholic Church.

Montague Summers

Much has been said about the barbaric excesses of the medieval inquisitors and rightly so, but less is known about those who choose to condemn magick (and witchcraft) in the most graphic terms in more recent, and – presumably - enlightened times. Only the fact that we no longer live trapped in a morass of superstition, ignorance and fear (plus of course a much more enlightened legal system) prevented them from inciting new witch-hunts with their attendant hysteria, fear and butchery.

Nevertheless, a few of these malicious zealots were still around, and one such man was Augustus Montague Summers, another exorcist and hammer of demonic forces. He was born in April 1880, the youngest of seven children of a prosperous banking family in Bristol, England. His early schooling was unremarkable, but he went on to study theology at the prestigious Trinity College located in Cambridge with the intention of becoming a priest in the Church of England.

He continued his training at Lichfield College and in 1908 achieved the minor rank of deacon in the Anglican Church. He did not receive any further promotions in the church, which may have been due to his abiding interest in Satanism. However, his interest in the subject, and actually practising it, were two entirely different things and should have been no impediment, but the rumours of his alleged interest in young boys certainly was. He was tried on charges of this nature, but was eventually found not guilty and acquitted. That said, his first published work in 1907, *Antinous*, dealt with the debased subject of pederasty. It seems strange that it is only now that effective legislation is in place to prevent any of these perverts having any contact with children.

Perhaps it reflected the hypocritical values of his times where many things were swept under the carpet to maintain the public façade of religious respectability and decency. Unfortunately, as already mentioned by Terry Stokes, it is also something that still bedevils the Catholic Church to this day, and has been highlighted by - at the time of writing - the evidence of an ongoing cover-up by the Church in Ireland during the late 20th Century when it evidently put its own reputation before the interests of children abused by its priests in that country. The severity of the issue also forced Pope Benedict XIV to issue a letter of public apology.

In 1909 Summers converted to Roman Catholicism and began to adopt the garb and manner of a priest in that religion which, given his theological training and the similarity between the two faiths, would have been relatively straightforward. It is here that we should look more closely at his actions, because there is considerably more to this than meets the eye. Yes, he did convert to Catholicism and adopted the extravagant soubriquet of Father Alphonsus Jesus-Mary Augustus Montague Summers, but this conversion was not into the mainstream Catholic Church, this was the aforementioned schism called 'The Old Catholic Church'.

Tellingly, among its differences with the Catholic Church is its acceptance of homosexuality as an acceptable lifestyle, which at that time was almost unheard of. The Old Catholic Church was founded during the 1870s in Germany as a result of the announcement of papal infallibility by the First Vatican Council in 1869-70 and took the name, *'The Union of Utrecht of Old Catholic Churches'*. Although it has no formal connection with the Holy See it does maintain contact with, and share many of, the ideas of the Anglican Communion.

The beliefs of the Old Catholic Church differ from the much less liberal and conservative Church of Rome in its already mentioned views on homosexuality, the ordination of women priests, which it has done since 1996, and its refusal to condemn artificial contraception, preferring instead to leave it up to the individual couple. From this it is not unreasonable to assume that Summers could more easily identify with the liberal attitude to homosexuality and therefore would feel better disposed to a church like this. However he also became a member of a secret society called *'The Order of Chaeronea'*, which may give a clearer understanding of his motives in joining the Old Catholic Church and of course to the other charges laid against him. George Cecil Ives founded the Order of Chaeronea in 1897 with the intention of promoting homosexuality with a cultural and spiritual ethos, a concept, which at that time was anathema to the general public.

Ives realised that there was little chance of the homosexual lifestyle being even close to acceptable in that era, so he decided to cultivate it secretly and in this way create an environment where homosexuals could mix and socialise with less fear of discovery and the consequent possibilities of ruin and probable imprisonment. To this end, he invented an elaborate set of rituals and initiations on similar lines to the Freemasons and other quasi-secret organisations that used signs and handshakes.

Another thing that also strikes a resonant chord with Freemasonry was the development of a sign-word, in this case, 'AMRRHMO', which finds a close parallel with Masonic term, 'HTWSSSTKS', which is often found stamped on Masonic pennies. HTWSSSTKS, the original meaning of which is supposedly lost, is remembered by the mnemonic, 'Hiram The Widows Son Sent Soon To King Solomon' or variants thereof. The meaning of the mnemonic, 'AMRRHMO', is unknown.

The keen interest that Summers apparently had in homosexuality and his possible paedophile inclinations aside, two of the things best known about him were his, at the time unique, translation of the odious Dominican witch finding manual, the *Malleus Malleficorum*, and the publication of his best known work, *The History of Witchcraft and Demonology*. (1926, reprinted in 1969). This was followed by a succession of works such as *The Geography of Witchcraft*, (1927) *A Popular History of Witchcraft* (1937) and *Witchcraft and Black Magic* (1946). Summers was absolutely convinced that all witches, black or white, were irredeemably in league with Satan, and his narrow definition of witchcraft provided no niceties of distinction between Wiccans, shamans, pagans and Satanists.

As far as he was concerned they were one and the same thing, and thoroughly deserved everything coming to them and he was especially enthusiastic about the horrors of the Inquisition. Some, probably apocryphal, stories have hinted that he had a remit from a shadowy organisation within the Catholic hierarchy to seek out, expose and excoriate witchcraft at every opportunity, which of course he did, although this was almost certainly entirely of his own volition. Summers wrote that witches embodied every foul and perverse passion known to man, that they were the epitome of evil, they were poisoners, worshippers of Satan, blasphemers, rapists, charlatans, bawds and abortionists.

He cultivated an air of mystery about himself and in appearance Summers was never less than striking, and frequently walked around wearing a cloak with his long silvery hair worn almost like a wig, while his fingers gleamed with his many jewelled rings. Oddly enough he did not adopt clerical garb all that often, and when he did it was purely for effect. In spite of his short stature, he generated considerable charisma and people who met him were frequently in awe, something that he used to his advantage. The former wartime member of the British intelligence service and author of many novels on black magick, Dennis Wheatley, said quite categorically that

Summers '*Inspired him with fear*'.

It has been suggested that Wheatley based the character, the enigmatic Canon Copley-Style, in his extremely influential and alarming novel (later released as a film), *The Devil Rides Out*, on Summers. In addition to his self-appointed role as an implacable foe of witchcraft and other evil doings, in common with Sean Manchester, Montague Summers also developed a keen interest in vampires and werewolves and espoused an unshakable belief in the reality of both of these legendary creatures. He went on to produce three books devoted to them, *The Vampire, His Kith and Kin* (1928), *The Vampire in Europe* (1929) and *The Werewolf* (1933).

In the course of his occult researches it was inevitable that Summers should come into contact with the legendary occultist Aleister Crowley, which he did, and against all expectations both men developed a friendship and mutual respect, meeting regularly to discuss and air their totally different viewpoints. On second glance perhaps it is not so surprising after all, since both of them were equally capable of plumbing the depths of the pit in their studies, both were extremely knowledgeable in their respective fields, and both had strange sexual proclivities. In addition, it is a fair bet that both men had grossly inflated egos and these meetings would probably allow them to strut and preen and demonstrate their knowledge. This same ego-driven vanity is also why both enjoyed, and deliberately cultivated, a high public profile. It should come as no surprise to learn that at one point Aleister Crowley attempted to set up his own religion using the title of '*Crowleyanity*'.

Right until he died in August 1948, the year after Crowley, Summers continued his vehement denunciation of magick and witchcraft while promoting the magickal beliefs of his church. He never faltered in his open admiration for the Inquisition and stoutly defended their record of brutality, murder and oppression; it was, after all, carried out with the best of intentions and sanctified in the name of God.

There can be little doubt that had Summers been born a few centuries earlier he would have equalled and even surpassed the efforts of such arch-Inquisitors as Dominic de Guzman and Tomas de Torquemada in his efforts to cleanse the planet from his narrow interpretation of sin. Thankfully he was not. As a last and possibly not too surprising word about Summers, there were suggestions that on December the 24th 1918 he conducted a Black Mass assisted by two young men. This assertion, if true, hints the man was either a dedicated researcher seeking to discover whether magick of this kind actually did produce results, or as the hypocritical pederast that he really was.

So there we have it, two men convinced of their mission to remove vampires, whether real or not, from the face of the earth. However, might they just have been on to something? Without wishing to delve too deeply into a real nest of vipers, it has been suggested that, in line with the rationale behind Chaos Magick, certain things, wishes if you like, can be made real by concentrating on them. They are called 'Tulpas' and are a part of the techniques and lore of Tibetan Buddhism. Is it possible that, given the high profile of fictional vampires in our society today that we might actually create one through sheer 'thought pressure'? The answer to this is unknown, but perhaps we should start looking closely at some of the reports of strange happenings and sightings in the pages of newspapers, the truth, as was repeatedly mentioned in the TV series the *X Files*, might indeed just be out there.

PART TWO

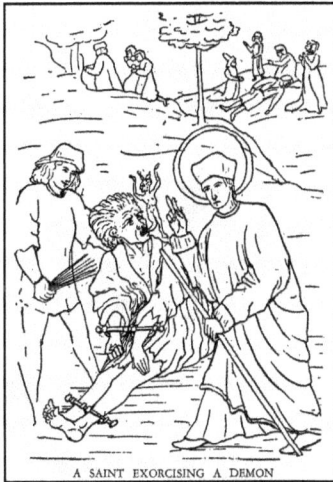

A SAINT EXORCISING A DEMON

Chapter 21
A Remote Exorcism

I n this section we will look at two very recent examples of what were effectively exorcisms and in which I had the opportunity to become personally involved. The first of these was done with no physical contact between me, the mediums (although I have previously met and worked with them) and the affected person; this is something akin to 'remote healing' and in this case was apparently eventually effective. I should emphasise 'eventually' here because it took more than one attempt to bring about a satisfactory result. One of the things about this case was that as far as the lady being affected was concerned this was the work of a poltergeist and this is how she describes it. At the time, in order not to inflame an already alarming situation, it was probably best that she continued to believe that, because in fact this was possession by any other name. However as the case progressed it became possible to reveal a little more of the background.

One of the main differences was that it was the possession of a place rather than a person, although it was a person, an old lady in fact, who had inadvertently created the situation. The details of the case also clearly show that there is precious little difference between poltergeist attacks and the symptoms of possession because they both react in a similar manner to attempts at removing them. The distances involved were quite remarkable too because the possession occurred in Mexico, I was in central Scotland and the medium was in London. It also shows that there does not always have to be face-to-face contact between all the interested parties, and that the barrier between the physical and non-physical may be extremely thin and permeable.

One of the most potentially alarming and frightening spiritual events that a human being can experience is the outbreak of paranormal activity in their home. There is usually no obvious rhyme or reason regarding why it occurs, but occasionally it can manifest in displays of apparently blind and pointless malice and damage. The range of classic phenomena can include everything from unexplained noises, smells, items being hurled around to untraceable voices etc. These events can occur in any order and in any combination, but in spite of this there is no obvious reason why any particular individual should be chosen to have this inflicted on them. In this case there was a boy in his late teens, but this in itself is not a viable reason because the phenomenon frequently occurs in locations where there no children and like many examples of the paranormal there is no consensus view. Besides, none of the explanations can satisfactorily demonstrate the mechanism behind it, i.e. so called 'spirit energy' being converted into mechanical force

The person on the receiving end of the unwelcome attention is an expatriate American citizen, Ms Terry Graham, who currently lives in Guadalajara in Mexico. Initially at least she had no idea why this should have occurred to her, and she has courageously allowed me to set out her account of the events and what we tried to do to control and defuse the situation. Much of what is here is told (with permission) in Terry's own words because they were so well and succinctly put that there was almost no need to paraphrase or change anything. However, where some alterations have been made this was only in the interests of simplicity because, as is the nature of email conversations, some of the wording was repeated and only served to confuse an already complex issue. The American spelling and terminology used by Terry is verbatim and has been left 'as is'.

Two other people who feature prominently in this account are a talented physical medium, the London based Patrick McNamara and Karl Fallon who is an IT specialist, but also a psychically talented individual in his own right who records the séances and other experiments conducted by Patrick. These recordings are usually displayed on their extremely informative, open-minded and surprisingly well-researched website, www.Ghostcircle.com. I have had the good fortune to work with Karl and Patrick on a previous occasion when conducting a remarkable experiment in physical mediumship approximately 30 metres underground in a former Cold War government command centre located near St Andrews in Scotland. The facility, which thankfully was never used in anger, is currently operated as a tourist attraction and has been preserved exactly as it would have been while in use.

First Contact

I first received an email from Terry Graham in July 2010 describing a series of unnerving events taking place in her home. The occurrences, and the unsettling effects they had on Terry and her son, prompted her to make contact with me. She had been experiencing an escalating series of unwelcome phenomena in her home for around two years beginning in 2008, which originally manifested in the form of damage to her furniture and the very fabric of the house itself.

What follows is a sequential account of our communications over a period of several months; the observations of Patrick and Karl are also included. Incidentally, as previously mentioned, for obvious reasons the spelling used by Terry is American and in each case where appropriate the advice, comments and observations made by Terry, Patrick and Karl are prefixed either (T) for Terry, (P) for Patrick or (K&P) for Karl and Patrick and (B) for me: her first account reads as follows. The first email arrived on the 21st of June 2010:

> (T) I am pretty sure that I have a poltergeist problem. I have an 84 year old aunt stricken with Alzheimer's who, despite her claims of independence, was compelled to come and live with me after having been abandoned by her son. After some months of living in my home things became mysteriously damaged. At first it was small; like chipped picture frames and broken corners on furniture and later the stonework around the house began to re-arrange into ugly formations and finally began to disappear. This has been going on for about a year and a half.
>
> Now the paint on the walls is dripping and slowly being removed from the walls, many of which are returning to their original colors despite the fact that the entire house was recently painted. I also have frequent black/brown slashes on the walls. My question is, short of an exorcism, how can I resolve this problem? My aunt has been in a nursing home for the past 6 months and the strange phenomena continue. I have had priests come to the house and many other "spiritual types" to no avail. What on earth can I do? Please help me if you can. Any advice you can offer would be well appreciated. Thank you.

This email arrived without any preamble and literally 'out of the blue', there was absolutely no input or prompting on my part and at first I was dubious regarding both the validity of the writer (initially, because of the name, Terry, I had no idea that this came from a woman) and her story.

My first reply was non-committal, merely requesting some background information and detail regarding the type of phenomena allegedly taking place. I also asked where she found my name, and if there had been any ordained priests or other clergymen involved, plus other mainly general questions; the quite lengthy answer came almost by return email.

> (T) Thank you for responding. Yes, I had a priest come, but he only blessed the house. Every rite and ritual in the country has been performed (except an outright exorcism) and there has been no change. Aside from the damage to the furniture and especially to the stonework (which is being cut into smaller and smaller pieces) the experience began with a mild odor of excrement. I could always tell when "it" was present because of the odors. The plants began to die, but except for two which finally withered completely, the rest have recovered. Twice after "riddance" ceremonies were performed in the house I found dead birds in my driveway, but this may have been coincidental. Then the black slashes on the walls began to be accompanied by a grimy feel about the house and windows. I also have small nicks and 'dings' in the walls, especially on the marble furniture.
>
> I have (I had) a small rock garden in back of the house and the rocks were once quite large with bamboo plants growing in the centre. It was quite a struggle finding and

bringing them all to the house. Most of the rocks have been reduced in size rather dramatically, so carrying them out won't be much of a problem. Now the paint is melting off the walls. When I wake in the morning there are drippings of paint in various parts of the house and the original colors on the walls, which were ghastly hues of blue, pink and green (covered over long ago) by 4 or 5 coats of off-white paint, have begun to return. The patches of the repair work are all now showing through.

Finally, I do have intermittent days of peace, but I am alerted to its return by the incessant clicking. The clicks move from one area of the room to another with lightening fast speed. Sometimes the clicks are low and soft and at other times they are quite loud, often startling me from sleep. I hope this information helps. At first I was afraid, terribly afraid, but now I am taking things in my stride. From my reading of events I thought it might simply disappear suddenly (in the manner in which it came) but after nearly two years and incredible damage to my home, I need help to figure this out. I found your name and contact on the Internet. I am in Guadalajara, Mexico. Mostly no one answers or they challenge my experience as possible lies because what I am describing does not sound familiar to them. I'm not sure how we would be able to meet, but I would be willing to call you anywhere in the world.

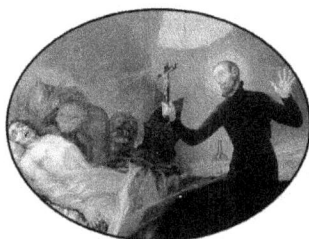

Chapter 22
So, What to Do?

n a situation like this it would have been ideal to meet Terry and inspect the house as it would have allowed me to inspect the location where the alleged phenomena were occurring. More importantly in cases like these it is extremely helpful to actually meet with the person involved, because the way in which they react to gentle but pertinent questioning can sometimes help to define whether the case is genuine, or perhaps due to personal issues that the person might have. Unfortunately, in a few cases the responses (and body language) resulting from face to face meetings can make it clear that the person is simply telling lies, although lying serves no useful purpose other than as a possible attention-seeking ploy. This is one of the inherent problems with investigations of this kind, because it is not up to the investigator to judge why they are being lied to, but only to make an assessment based on the information they are given.

As it turned out, because this was occurring in Mexico, the sheer distance and expense involved was enough to cancel out any reasonable prospect of travelling to the scene, so the only way forward was by opening a detailed email conversation. In retrospect with this particular case, although face-to-face is preferable, the 'hands off' approach possibly offered the best way to deal with the situation since it gave me a chance to consider and weigh the options open to all concerned. Another advantage of an 'arms length' assessment was that I could evaluate the content and implications of my replies at leisure, since off-the-cuff, or unguarded remarks made during a face-to-face interview can have unintended and unsuspected consequences. I have had personal experience of what can happen on investigations when an inappropriate (albeit innocent) remark or observation is made by someone present, most likely one of the investigators, to whomever is experiencing issues with something possibly paranormal. The potential effects can be devastating to the wellbeing of the person having the experiences, and the resulting negativity can be difficult to dispel.

Of course, in the case of Terry Smith the additional benefit was that I was able to participate in a remote exorcism, although none of that would have been possible were it not for the fact that Terry appeared to be extremely pragmatic and level-headed about the whole situation. One factor that I did find unusual was that no-one in Mexico had been able to help, but perhaps she was asking the wrong people. At this point, based on what had been said so far, I sent an email asking some detailed questions, and what follows is a condensed version of that email conversation.

(B) I do not think this is a poltergeist (but I could be wrong), if anything it sounds like something from the lower astral realm, it's certainly malicious enough. However, they can be dealt with effectively, but it's a pity that the priests will not perform a full exorcism under the auspices of the 'Rituale Romanum' (RR) which is the traditional and approved Roman Catholic ritual of exorcism, because they can, will and should if you can convince them that you need it done.

(T) I am not a Roman Catholic, but I can try and speak with a priest and see what happens. I certainly don't have anything to lose.

(B) They tend to be a bit reluctant because it's a hassle and it involves receiving the express permission of the local bishop. The questions remains, have you explicitly asked them to do this? Because if you happened to be a Catholic they have a duty of care for you spiritual needs (and safety); have you tried a shaman or even a local spiritualist group/church?

(T) Yes, I have had many spiritualists (I don't remember a shaman specifically) come to the house and perform various ceremonies. Nothing really has worked. A day or two of peace and then right back to the malicious damage.

At this point, based on what she had said I decided to offer to send her a copy of the RR. I also advised her that although it is supposed to be conducted by an ordained priest it can also be used by a layperson, although she might well need an assistant. I also informed two excellent mediums (Patrick and Karl) with whom I had previously worked to see what they thought and I promised to keep Terry appraised of their opinions.

(T) *I would appreciate the text of the RR; I certainly don't have anything to lose by trying. I suppose that my 18 year old son could be my assistant if I need one. I am very anxious to hear what the mediums might think. I spoke with one here in Mexico who would not even come to my house because she was afraid.*

Fully aware that this might sound like a foolish question, I asked her if she had deeply held religious beliefs and if she had tried just asking or praying for it to go?

(T) *I believe in God, but I am not a big fan of organized religion. I often say a prayer to Saint Michael asking for deliverance. I have not asked it to go away (yet) because I read somewhere that it should never be directly addressed and therefore I haven't, but I will if you think it is a good idea.*

I Cast Thee Out

I replied that they were often happy if human beings recognised that existence, although depending on the entity giving it a name can empower it. She replied as follows:

> (T) *My son and I often joke about the situation, but most of the time we act like nothing is happening and we certainly never talk to it.*

I then asked if the entity had ever actually spoken or communicated with her or her son directly, and if she had ever actually seen any of these phenomena occurring?

> (T) *No, it has never spoken to us and I have never seen any of the phenomena actually occurring.*

I replied by asking if things were ok in the evening and changed in the morning (or *vice versa)?*

> (T) *Odd things happen during both the day and night, but I never see them happening. It is mostly when we are asleep or not at home. There does not seem to be a whole lot of difference between day and night as far as that goes, although of late, it is around much less during the day. Something else that I forgot to mention is that it removes paint and varnish from things. One morning I woke up and even my nail polish was gone! Also, many of our electrical appliances burned out and had to be replaced. We now unplug most things before we go to bed.*

What follows is, once again, a condensed version of the conversation.

> (B) *The big issue here is that I am in Scotland and we cannot talk face to face (and neither can the mediums,) also my wife and I are off on a short vacation starting on Saturday.*

> (T) *After nearly two years of this torment, a few more weeks couldn't possibly make a difference. Please enjoy your time away but PLEASE don't forget me.*

> (T) *On a final note: a medium once claimed that he channelled it and the entity claimed that he was called up by my aunt to help her return to her home in Arizona. I cannot say how true that is or isn't, BUT everyone who has come to my home has said that my aunt dealt in the black arts (Voodoo, Santeria etc.) and this disturbance is due to her. Just so you know, I had no idea of any such dealings on her part and I myself have zero connection to the occult world. Thank you for the assurances and thank you for not signalling that you think I might be crazy. Every word of what I am relating is true. Also, many of our electrical appliances burned out and*

had to be replaced. We now unplug most things before we go to bed.

(B) The mention of electrical equipment failure is not unknown in these cases and indicates something quite different and it does not involve any ill intentioned astral being either. So before we start involving some 'heavy stuff' let's consider a condition called 'electrical hypersensitivity' or EH (Google it) that may be causing these effects to occur. Look it up and see if any of the events you are experiencing line up with the symptoms of the condition. Let us know then we can take it further. There is a list of approx 25 questions that might shed further light on this, but I'd have to look them out. *Note: a list of these 25 questions is included at the end of the book*

At this point my wife and I went off on a short prearranged vacation, but gave our assurances to Terry that we were taking the case seriously, and as soon as we returned home we would resume. I also asked her if she had any photographs of the damage being caused by the unwanted 'visitor'. I also once again offered to send the text of the *'Rituale Romanum'* (RR), as already noted, although this is intended to be said by an ordained priest, in an emergency it can be used by laypeople too with some very minor alterations. I also cautioned her, warning that if used incorrectly it was just possible that the RR text could carry a slight element of personal risk to her and her son, but there were very few instances where this had happened. *Note, an English translation of the Rituale Romanum is also included at the end of the book*.*

By 'risk' I meant that although it should be safe enough, when dealing with this subject there are no givens and spiritual, psychological and perhaps even physical injury could occur, although any damage would most likely be to her property and its contents. I also strongly recommended that if she did want to proceed down that route she should keep trying to have a full-blown exorcism conducted by a properly trained and/or ordained person; and if that failed then I would send the ritual to her. I also asked her to consider allowing an Evangelical/Pentecostal type group conduct their version of an exorcism. I did warn her that, although worth a try, these can be extremely intense and tend to focus on the person rather than the property and warned her to be very wary. When my wife and I returned from our time away, this reply was waiting for us in the email in-box.

Chapter 23
The *Rituale Romanum*

This chapter opens with another conversation between Terry and me regarding my queries about both using the *Rituale Romanum* and relating to her aunt.

(T) Not sure about the RR text. I think I would be afraid to do that. I will get a Catholic friend to help me with a local parish priest.

(B) Do you mean that your friend will ask the priest to consider an exorcism? He (the priest) will not be anxious to do this for the reasons already stated. You would really have to convince him, but even then he might only want to do a house blessing. Some of the evangelical groups might help, but like I say, they can be a bit, shall we say, 'intense' and might scare the hell out of you. They tend to assume that the person and not the house is possessed. Personally I have little time for them.

(T) As I said, I have had a number of "Ghostbuster" types in the house who performed various rites and rituals. Right now, I would not be able to say if they were mediums or psychics because I wasn't smart enough to ask. However, in retrospect, I think they were either psychics or clairvoyants. I do not have any knowledge of anyone in my family ever having more than a passing acquaintance with the occult. Tarot cards, strange dreams etc. My aunt was nick-named the "dreamer" because she would dream things that would often later come true.

(B) It sounds as if she may have some kind of inadvertent 'wild talent'

(T) Yes, during one of my visits to my aunt's nursing home several months ago, by chance she was having a very lucid moment so I asked her about any association with the black arts/occult. She said that she did not remember, but knew that she had done a lot of evil things in her lifetime.

(B) This all depends on what they were; evil has many faces and even more contexts and interpretations. Can she remember what occurred, but keep in mind that there is evil and there is spiritual evil, two different things. Like I said, it's all about perception and context

(T) I then asked her if she had ever been afraid of the power of God and her answer was surprising. She said, "No, I have never been afraid of God and I am now ready to face whatever it is I have to face." I wept and prayed for her the entire week.

(B) That must have been extremely upsetting for you, but there is no real reason why she should be afraid, that rather depends on her personal spiritual paradigm. BTW, have you had the time to look into the possibility of EH being factor here?

(T) Neither one of us appears to have any of the indicating markers.

(B) Ok, but try spreading the search out a little, try looking up 'Albert Budden and the 25 questions', or associate the name with 'poltergeist machine' and 'John Hutchison', the results might really surprise you.

(T) A while back the phones used to ring randomly without anyone being there, the phones themselves eventually died, my son lost his desk top computer and we burned out one relatively new and one brand new printer. Conversely we never unplug the fridge or stove at night and we have never had a problem with them. Yet.

(B) Just a thought, but is your home near power lines, microwave transmitters, radio/TV masts, electrical substations, emergency services, taxi firms, or anything of that kind? (I asked this question because these factors have a direct effect on the syndrome of EH and at this stage I believed that this might be the cause and was therefore worth pursuing, as it happens I never did get an answer. Unfortunate but it is in the unpredictable nature of these investigations).

(T) Photos: The attached photos are indicative of the type of damage generally found in my home. Even though I recently had the house remodeled, the appearance of the home is in run down condition and getting worse. Each photo is numbered and a brief explanation is below.

1. The left door is being shaved from the top and the right door is being shaved from the bottom.
2. Paint being peeled away from ceiling in bathroom
3. Paint being peeled away from underneath the glass
4. Paint oddly disappearing from side of sink
5. Brick arches in kitchen becoming disfigured
6. Damaged tile behind front gate near front door
7. Stone work on kitchen counter becoming stretched and disfigured
8. Nick in Formica in kitchen
9. Nick in corner of picture frame
10. Size of rocks in bamboo garden being reduced
11. Stone on steps being shaved away

12. Damage on tile in master bedroom
13. If you look closely you will see a set of black tracks in the stonework. It is common to see this throughout the house. Sometimes they are very dark and at other times they are a caramel color.
14. This type of nick is now everywhere throughout the house. Every single thing we own has been damaged in some way.

I should tell you that with regard to the photographs (a selection of these are included in the picture plates section), in my opinion the damage shown appears typical of that which occurs in any household as part of normal wear and tear. I said this to Terry and she agrees, but she is adamant that despite this, the damaged is caused by the entity and is still occurring.

Electrical Hypersensitivity

It's as well to pause here to look briefly at the phenomenon of electrical hypersensitivity because some of the traits in this syndrome can emulate those frequently seen in outbreaks of poltergeist activity. The unusual happenings were first noted by the Canadian electromagnetic researcher, John Hutchison, who at the time was living in Vancouver, Canada. As he conducted a series of experiments using a wide variety of equipment including Tesla coils, radar antennae, microwave emitters and assorted kinds of radio equipment, he noted that small items and artefacts made of all kinds of material, metallic and non-metallic, ferrous and non-ferrous, would spontaneously rise into the air and float around. This went on until the electronic equipment was switched off. In addition to this, mysterious winds and draughts would suddenly appear and small fires would occur, fortunately none of them serious.

Since Hutchison lived in an apartment block at the time, this type of activity was not popular with his neighbours who regarded him as a kind of mad professor, but the last straw was the loss of all the channels on their TV sets. This was something that occurred regularly and they could pinpoint it directly to Hutchison and his experiments. It should be pointed out that John Hutchison is entirely self-taught, and his equipment is either homemade or had been bought as surplus from various ex-government and ex-military sources. Hutchison's apartment is literally jammed to the ceiling in every room with equipment of this kind and it has more or less taken over. The balcony of his apartment is likewise festooned with fully functioning antennae of various kinds and none of them intended for domestic use.

At any rate, Hutchison's neighbours eventually called the police who arrived at his apartment and confiscated the majority of his equipment; although he did get it back eventually. Aside from the nuisance to his neighbours, the experimenter became fascinated by the range of phenomena he continually observed during his experiments. He decided to contact the Canadian government to share his findings, and to see if they could come up with an explanation. The Canadian government took note and carried out a series of tests, but refused to divulge its findings saying that it was not in the interests of national security.

He then contacted the US government who also investigated, and - as with their Canadian counterparts - would not release their findings. I have also investigated this phenomenon under the US Freedom of Information Act and was met with continual official denials from the US Army Intelligence Dept based at Ft Meade in Maryland, USA. When I persisted and showed them copies of material originating from their department they eventually said sorry and directed me the Los Alamos National Laboratory (LANL). They in turn did have records of what occurred, but redirected me to Ft Meade again. Eventually the authorities at Ft Meade said they could not be of any further help as they claimed to have 'lost' the file, which, given the nature of their work, seems extremely careless of them.

Chapter 24
Further Developments

As part of the ongoing email conversation I asked Terry if anything of value had been damaged, or if the damage was confined to the fabric of the house and garden. I had also asked most of the usual questions regarding the area the house was built on and if she had been able to get any answers from the groups she had contacted. By that I mean that when investigating an alleged haunting or poltergeist manifestation it is advisable to uncover as much background information about the premises as possible. It is assumed by some researchers that old buildings might in same way 'absorb' or 'record' impressions of events that had occurred there in the past in their structure. This is just one of many theories that have developed around this most ephemeral of phenomena and it is as valid (or wide of the mark) as many of the rest: in any event this is her reply.

(T) Yes, many valuables have been damaged. Most of the antique marble furniture has now been severely chipped or scarred and a very expensive set of granite canopic jars have been seriously damaged. The nose was broken off a figure and an arc shaped piece was cut from the head stone. Arc-shaped damage is common. Many of the stones have little arc shaped cuts in them and at first the damage to the plants involved little arc shaped cuts on the leaves. Now, most of the valuable art objects have been put away. It does not seem to bother things once they have been put away.

(T) No, I really don't know anything about the land the house is built on. We pretty much lived in harmony (two years) until my aunt came one and a half years ago, but that was also the same time as the beginning of the massive remodelling project. At the time we brought her here, there was no real plan. I travelled to Arizona to visit her, realized that she was no longer able to live alone and brought her to Mexico within days.

As the reader may have already gathered, Terry's aunt suffers from the distressing and debilitating affliction of dementia. The condition has the added dimension of affecting all concerned, because the family is watching their loved one gradually, but remorselessly, disappearing before their eyes and they are powerless to stop it.

The only care available is mainly palliative rather than anything capable of causing any reversal of the condition.

(T) We at first considered that maybe we had disturbed some ancient resident who was there long before we came along, but most of the psychics/clairvoyants/mediums said, "no". I forgot to mention that we went through a water stage where we would suddenly come upon puddles of water in the house. They were quite random but mostly found on the roof in a small room that we use for laundry. Often in the middle of the living room and frequently in the guest bedroom we would randomly come upon puddles of water. Now it is un-levelling the furniture as in the armoire doors or the legs of the chairs.

Much of the furniture is uneven on its legs or has one leg shorter than the other. In the beginning I had a brick wall in my office. The spaces between the brick filled by the grout kept getting wider and wider. After a while, without exaggeration, the spacing between each brick was about 2 inches. It looked REALLY weird so I had the wall covered over in a white stone that did not require grout. The stone itself is now being shaved across the surface. There are never pieces of stone on the floor, but there is always dust left behind from the process. Whatever the process is, if you wipe your hand across the affected stone, it is always dusty despite several applications of varnish.

As for the paint, it is definitely not a manufacturing problem. Unless you want to count entire coats of paint plus some of the wall disappearing overnight as the manufacturer's problem! The paint has disappeared coat by coat until presently you can see all the former colors of blue and pink which I painted over in the first place. Also you can see the ragged edges where the paint has disappeared. Not sure how to say this exactly, but there are often lumps on the walls where the entity might have been standing and all around that point the wall is reduced by the thickness of the paint coat. This is happening to the paint on both the inside and outside walls of the house.

As for what I may have said to whom...I honestly don't remember. What is salient in my mind is the fact that every single person eventually gravitated to the roof as the focal point of the negative energy. My roof has a high wall and has been turned into a garden with a wide array of plants. At first the plants were being cut down and ripped out by the roots. Little arc shapes were on most leaves. As mentioned earlier, the plants started to die. I was grief stricken. I have a small table in the middle of the plants for reading etc. and that was badly chipped as well. Most of the strange water appeared in the room next to the plants. I was desperate to save my plants. Suddenly the plants recovered and the water on the roof and elsewhere in the house disappeared as suddenly as it appeared. If the people who came here were clueless, they all identified the center of negative energy as the exact same place. The roof!

Finally, nothing that I am aware of has been moved or thrown around. We once could not find a $100 bill, but I doubt that that is related. I have a bracelet with turquoise stones in it and a couple of the stones were strangely cut so I put it away. I have noticed that it never touches the gold or silver jewellery. I used to drive a 10-year old Volvo. The sun roof mysteriously started leaking. The stitching on the leather seats was also cut loose. I have several skylights in the house and the one over my bed leaks furiously during the rain despite multiple attempts to repair it. I suppose that we can say that many things are coincidental, but taken as a totality; with hundreds of points of damage all within the last 18 months...I doubt it.

By this point I had contacted Patrick and Karl and asked for their input and opinion, I also informed Terry about my decision, and she seemed delighted that she was at last being taken seriously and I can sympathise with her. I have met many people who were almost at their wits end between having to cope with the unwelcome and unwanted results of hauntings and/or poltergeist activity, and trying to find someone to help them deal with it. At that time both Patrick and Karl had requested that I did not reveal their identities or website address to Terry, although as the case progressed that changed. Incidentally, the appearance of the puddles of water is another classic attribute of events such as these and there is no obvious reason for it, although it *may* be connected to a possible energy source that serves the entities.

I also informed her that after thinking about what she had written there was one element that rang a faint alarm bell that had to be eliminated. It concerned the person who helped with the housework and cleaning around the house. I asked the following questions to rule out the obvious, i.e. was it possible that the person she was employing was the cause of what was happening? Were they there before this started happening, or just while her aunt was in the house and right up to the present?

(T) The woman who works for me has been with me for the last couple of years, but absent a good part of that time due to the illness and subsequent death of her mother. She was only in the household for about two weeks when my aunt was here and then left for about one year to tend to the issues in her own family as primary care-giver. She recently returned about 3 months ago but my aunt left for the nursing home long before Irma (the domestic) returned.

The physical medium who was now involved suggested that we might try a remote exorcism/cleansing, and asked that I remain the primary contact so I respected his wishes. I then asked Terry to suggest a suitable time and date to attempt an exorcism; this had to take into account the time difference.

(T) Just let me know what makes sense for you and him. I will comply with whatever seems best for the two of you. Sometime between now and Saturday would probably be best because my vacation ends and I return to work on Monday. That is to imply that I could stay up all night up until then to accommodate an hour that was convenient for you given the time difference.

(B) As you will recall I attached the text of the RR in a previous email just in case and to clarify a little after some further research I am sure it can be used by the laity, but hopefully you will not have to.

(T) In the text, what do the V and R stand for? I am guessing that R is for respondent but I really don't know. I have to be sure about all this stuff in case I become unusually eager to launch myself into the depths of the unknown! Sorry Brian...I have one last question. What happens if we just pack up and move? Does the problem remain in the house? Does the problem go with us wherever we go because of the commitment to my aunt? The thought of leaving my home would break my heart but I would do it IF that would solve the problem. What do you think?

(B) I advise that if possible you try to stay calm and the candles be lit before attempting anything, but this type of prayer (which is what it is) should be a used as last resort, if possible let your priest contact get back to you. As it turned out this never occurred.

(T) It is sort of like the movie, *The Others*, if you have seen it.

(B) I see what you mean.

(T) How could or would someone use this type of energy? What would they be doing with it? Are my son and I involved in some way?

(B) I would need the medium to make a call on that, I have no doubt that he will. Besides, if you are involved it is by default more than anything else. Incidentally it might be helpful if we used something called the Rosslyn Frequencies while we try this. I'll send you a sound file, oh, and you will probably need some candles, three of them.

(T) I have checked on the Internet for the Rosslyn Frequencies and there seems to be a movie but the frequencies themselves seem to be very disconcerting. I will definitely watch the movie just to satisfy my curiosity, but are the frequencies these disconcerting sounds? I went to your web site, but I was unable to figure it out. What exactly do you want me to do? Listen? Watch? I bought three of the religious candles today. All I need is the time and place and the specifics of the frequencies. My son and I spoke about it in detail this afternoon and he agrees that we may very well be getting at the root of it. Thanks.

(B)You are most welcome, I will send the frequencies as wav files but do keep in mind that this is not a precise science and we might achieve very little, but as I said it will not worsen the situation. I have sent this reply to the medium. BTW, try not to worry, the medium will tell you exactly what you have to do and when to do it.

Chapter 25
Patrick Expresses an Opinion

It was becoming increasingly clear that the unfortunate Terry was losing her former resolve and now appeared to be quite agitated and 'edgy' about what was occurring, I had also being supplying Patrick and Karl with as much information as I could. This included forwarding Terry's emails to them (with her knowledge and approval), and what follows is Patrick's assessment based on these emails, and his own usually first class intuition.

Patrick's Assessment

(P) The son was around sixteen years old when this happened. The aunt with Alzheimer's disease is wide open and allowing dimensional doorways to open and close. There is a woman who lived (Liani or Liana) in the house and she didn't like the new changes that were made to the house. She used the son and the Alzheimer aunt to start things off, using the expanded and open aura of the aunt. There is a dimensional doorway or doorways that have been opened by the aunt. There is also a spirit present which seems to be a woman, it sounds like Liana, has created a time rift and she is not happy with the new changes so she is trying to destroy what she believes is poltergeist activity on HER side. It's a form of cross vibration where the spirit in the other dimension is very disturbed.

There are other entities who are helping focus this and the arrival of mediums and others to try "fix things" are actually helping to empower the energy to cause more trouble between the previous owner and the new owner. There are other lower astral spirits who are also using the aunt's aura to focus on the house as she is very open with her Alzheimer. Even though the aunt is not living there she is effectively thinking that she is still there. On top of this, some occultists are taking advantage of the situation and are also using the energy after visiting the house or hearing about it through word of mouth. The owner and her son are opening and closing the door due to their belief that there are dark forces around and they are thus empowering them even more.

I have a South American Indian, he just appeared now and he is talking to me. If they call on the elements of the sun and the earth and call on this guide, he is a dimensional doorway keeper; his name is Hotec of the old Indian tribes. He will help to close those dimensional doorways. The power of the mind is the important thing. I suggest that use of one of the frequencies may help as well; it is a case of if they believe that the doors can be closed then the doors will be closed. They are keeping them open. I suggest you send her one or two of the Rosslyn frequencies to play.

Tell her to light three candles, open all the doors and windows of the house, call on the Aztec guide 'Hotec', and get them [Terry and her son] to play some of your frequencies. If you can set or give a time that will do this then I can concentrate on the place at the same time and help out. We can do this as an experiment. We will try and close the dimensional doors on them. I believe it is a dimensional tear on at least two dimensions and maybe more. There is a 'door keeper' and he can look after her. Just as thought waves and ritualisation can produce different forms of energy, that energy can be manipulated to open or close down different dimensions.

After reading what Patrick had to say I sent the email to Terry

(B) Well, there you have it so far...I'm sure we can sort this out for you, or, if nothing, else have a damned good try at it, whatever, it shouldn't make it any worse'.

(T) You seem to understand more than anyone else I have spoken to. Based on what I have experienced, it makes sense. My son and I spoke about it in detail this afternoon and he agrees that we may very well be getting at the root of it. Thanks.

I was also entering a phase in the project where I experienced some frustration at acting as a 'middle man' in all this since my usual approach is to 'lead from the front'. This was, of course, due to the fact that the mediums had requested that I did not reveal their identities and their email addresses and, in particular, their website. In addition to this, I was also attempting to keep Terry calm as the date for the attempted exorcism drew closer and this involved answering her queries as best I could regarding the comments made by Patrick, and to some extent my own. It was the first time that I had some doubts over whether this was the best method of dealing with the events in Mexico. I should add that I had no doubts whatsoever that Patrick and Karl would do what they had to do, nor that Terry would carry out the instructions to the letter, but the doubts would not go away.

The EVP

Two days prior to conducting the exorcism Patrick suggested that we attempt to contact the entity, if that is what it was, by using a technique called 'electronic voice phenomenon', or EVP for short. In some circumstances this can by extremely successful, and involves the use of a tape recorder or other recording device. The questioner switches on the recorder, tape or digital - it makes no difference - and asks a simple question requiring only a yes or no answer. Sometimes it is more convenient to work out some kind of code that does not require any voice, such as one tap, or in the case of Terry a 'click' for yes, and two for no, much as the traditional method of 'taps' employed during séances.

I asked Terry if this was possible and she was agreeable to at least try, and the results, which were captured direct to her computer, arrived via MP3 files, each of five minutes duration. The results were not conclusive one way or another and on reflection it seemed as if she asked too many questions, and as a result received no readily audible answers. I advised her to try again, but this time to proceed more slowly and deliberately. A little later, having learned from her previous attempt, she was able to capture and record the 'clicks' and these files were sent as well. I thought that the sounds had a peculiar quality about them, they sounded strangely hollow, more like the tap one might expect knocking lightly on a thin piece of wood; this sound file was sent to Patrick and Karl who agreed with my assessment. Oddly enough, I had previously heard similar sounds during other investigations where poltergeist activity had been suspected, and they too had this odd, hollow timbre. Terry's comments on the EVP are set out below

(T) I am attaching the new recording that I made this morning. I could hear the clicks directly in front of me near the window at the time of the recording but there does not seem to be anything recorded. At least it appears that way to me. I have asked my son to ask the questions as well (in case it might prefer speaking to him) but now that he is home, it isn't. In any event, we will be ready tomorrow at 10pm (your time) and try again. Thank you and of course, thank the medium.

We will both try the EVP again this afternoon after we do our thing at 4pm. As for my friends, I have two very long term friends who are aware of the issues in the house. If the question is about the specifics of what will happen this afternoon, for example, then the answer is NO. I haven't brought it up. I have two workers in the house painting. Can they still be around at 4pm or should I dismiss them early? Well, there seemed to have been some movement in the first 25-30% of the recording and it was probably one of us moving around. It is the recording made while we were not home that is the most interesting. Lots of stuff going on in a supposedly empty house! Do you have a Messenger account. I think Messenger works as sort of an FTP so maybe I would have success transferring the file to you that way. Let me know.

Well, we did as instructed again and then immediately made the recordings. The clicks are quite clear on the recordings this time. They come up in a seemingly random manner but they are clearly there. On the "Terry" recording in the beginning when I ask, "Who are you?" there is a click. Then again when I ask, "Is there a reason you are destroying the stone?" Then we both went out and left the computer on play while we were gone. In the "As we left" recording you can hear the front door close and then we were gone. Then you can hear a street vendor yelling something and later our next door neighbors walking around or at least I think that is what it is. Then weird noises begin. My son says it is the refrigerator but it is waaaay to loud to be that. I think it is the motor (fan) on my computer but also there is a smaller more subtle noise underneath it. For a house that was supposed to be empty, there does seem to be a lot going on. The first recording I made is in a separate email.

1:27 click
4:35 click
6:30 click
6:48 my cell phone battery running down12:25 ? Maybe my computer
14:50 ? Maybe my computer
15:25 click
30:20 click33:07 click
36:10 click
 36:53 cell phone
1:51:45 really loud click, which often happens. Some hours later we return and eat some tacos and chat about a friend who is very sick and will return to the U.S. On another note, my son also tried to make a recording but the computer crashed both times as he tried. We both thought that was kind of strange.

Terry had sent these as MP3 files so I was able to download and listen to them, and also sent them to Patrick and Karl. This time the clicks were particularly clear.

Chapter 26
The First Exorcism: Aug 16th 2010

After much to-ing and fro-ing of emails a date was finally set for the exorcism attempt, which necessarily involved establishing a set of rules and a set procedure. Since Patrick was effectively in the driving seat regarding what was to happen, he obviously had to establish what he required, which was as follows. The account comes from Karl Fallon.

> (K) Maybe we can arrange it for tomorrow if possible. I thought at 9pm or 10pm UK time, which I guess is 3pm or 4pm, Mexico time being 6 hours behind us. Can you make and send her a 5 minute sample of the Gematria Equivalents tone on email (*see the section on the Rosslyn Frequencies at the end of the book*) ...All she needs to do is sit with her son, windows open doors open, light the three candles and play the tone for 3 minutes, one minute for each candle. Then ask for light to enter her house and say "I reject darkness and call upon the spirit guides for help, to fill the house with light." Then close each door and window in turn while asking to keep the light in the house. Once all are closed blow out the three candles. Done. We will do the rest from here.

After some last minute fine tuning the agreed time and date for the exorcism was reached; Mon, Aug 16, 2010 at 22:00 UK time which was 16:00 hrs Mexico time, what follows is a verbatim account supplied by Karl Fallon, one of the mediums involved.

Pre Ritual Preparations and the Build Up

> (P&K) We started to open a link with this lady by using her voice, which was recorded by her and played on an EVP conversation that was given to us by Brian Allan. Voice contact is important to help make a psychic link and it was fortunate that we had an EVP sent to us earlier in the day. We played the MP3 file for a short while before the ritual, which further strengthened the link. We began the process of connection about 9:50pm but did not start playing the tone until precisely 10pm as we agreed. We sat, one on either side of a table, which had candles and other items on it intended for use during the ritual. Within a matter of seconds of sitting

down we felt cold breezes coming from underneath the table. Patrick said he could hear the sound of birds wings beating in the air. A South American Indian presence appeared before Patrick and he could be described as either Aztec or Incan, it is 'Hotec' who we had encountered previously.

Just before we started playing the tones at 10pm, a very angry woman in spirit from the Mexican side linked with Patrick. She started talking about murder, and poison. There is a group of really negative spirits, negative energy, and they have banded together and are using the energies expressed in the house. They want fear, they want stress, and they want anxiety, they feed off of these energies. Patrick started feeling under attack from these nasty spirits so he called on his guardians for protection and to come near. He asked for a circle of light to be placed around the house in Mexico, he also asked for peace and light to enter into the house.

A very nasty and unpleasant man arrives in spirit; he is associated with this woman and along with her he has been causing trouble, the woman is powerful and almost certainly evil. Patrick asked for them to be separated. There is a curse associated with the whole situation, somebody has laid a curse. A very, very, powerful energy has been attached to this place and this person, the woman described previously, was murdered; probably poisoned. She was definitely murdered. She is really, really, negative and bitter. The woman has attracted a band of these negative entities to her: (Patrick is being physically attacked during this moment).

Patrick describes a man's face coming rushing up to him, the man is snarling and his face is contorted with hatred. The woman is there too and she was probably quite beautiful when younger, but her face is twisted now and it reflects her spiritual presence rather than physical beauty she once had. The name Roberto (Robert) is picked up. This whole situation is interconnected to Ivy (and Evey) and it needs to be released. The doorways need to be closed. The people in the house need to pray for peace in their own home and the spirits present will close the doorways for them. Their prayers will help. They have to close the door themselves and keep it closed.

The Ritual

It is now 10pm and Patrick begins the actual ritual process. The tone which is played in London will link with the same tone in Mexico. Patrick says a ritual candle prayer of the earth and of spirit to start the whole process. This will help remove the negative energies and start a pathway of forgiveness in Mexico. As the doorway between London and Mexico is now open, we begin closing the channels and doorways used by the dark entities in Mexico. As the tone is played the energy starts to vibrate both of our bodies. It could be described like a feeling of adrenaline where your whole body shakes. We are also using a red and blue light in the room and the lights start to dim and briefly pulsate by themselves.

As the connection between London and Mexico is now established the whole atmosphere seems to change and it seems like it is vibrating; the feeling is similar to standing close to a pneumatic drill which is in use. Looking at the three lit candles in front of us they are waving like snakes standing upright in the red and blue lit atmosphere. A cool breeze comes in from above and below and the table, which we have now placed our hands on, starts to vibrate. It then begins to move twice to the left in spurts and then to the right. Our hands are lightly touching the table, but still it moves. When Patrick briefly lifts his hands from the table, the table still moves by itself. Patrick feels energy pouring off of him, and I see that his hands begin to get physically thinner and his fingers looked longer, nearly twice as long as normal. This is exactly what we would see if we were conducting a physical mediumship circle; the table is still moving and tapping.

Now there is a strong smell of damp earth and the tone stops playing as we only set it for a duration of five minutes. We are now asking to close the doorway in Mexico. There is something quite dark that is still present, and it is standing behind me. Patrick sees the figure as a small boy, but he is not nice, it feels as if it may not be a boy but, instead, something taking the shape of one. Patrick believes he was one of the group of negative entities, but he is now separated from them. Patrick tries to remove him from the situation by allowing him into his aura and removing him with the help of his guides. I see an image of him now. He looks like a small, Native American Indian boy, he is not wearing a shirt and I can see his back; he has long black hair past his shoulder. Patrick now asks for the boy to be surrounded in light and he is taken away by two guides, he struggles fiercely but he is removed. I now see a long knife with a short handle. The handle looks wooden and the blade is not a well honed metal blade, but looks quite crude in appearance, like a small machete. I also see a pair of boots.

As soon as the boy is gone the whole atmosphere changes and it is so apparent that both of us feel much lighter and calmer. The lights in the room also went up. It was very tangible, changing from dark to light if you can describe it that way. Patrick again asks the guardians to uplift the family in Mexico, and give them light and peace. The most important thing now is that the family in Mexico remove the fear and anxiety in their minds and push these entities out. They have no right to be there and they should move on. By praying and thinking positively they can remove the energy. It's just like taking air from a balloon, and whole the situation will contract like a balloon too. At this point I see a guide appear over Patrick's face, it was a big man with a beard; a very full beard. He looked a bit like a cross between the actor Brian Blessed and the opera singer Luciano Pavarotti. It is briefly unsettling because Patrick does not have a beard.

At this point Patrick makes a few observations:

The tones and the red and blue light definitely help to channel the energy to the degree that you could physically see and feel the energy. The energy was similar to what we have seen before but more intense. The translucency of both physical and etheric objects is enhanced when the tone is played. The most important part now is their own belief, their self belief that they can clear the presences from the situation by themselves. The door needs to be closed by them as they are supplying the energy. Hopefully this will help them to bring these incidents to a closure but it is in their hands.

Patrick was of course absolutely correct and all we could do now was wait...and hope. Patrick phoned me at around 11pm after the ritual; this verbatim copy of what he said serves as a counterpoint and corroboration of what Karl had to say. Note that the entire ritual had been recorded on a digital video camera.

(P) I was extremely angry after the experimental ritual. There was absolute pandemonium in the houses on both sides of mine, and the occupants on the house at the rear decided to have a barbeque just to ramp up the irritation factor, it made concentrating difficult. Incidentally there is a shadow on the camera which we need to look at closely. Whatever we were trying to get rid of knew in advance and was doing it's best to cause a rift. It succeeded to a certain extent, but I also succeeded too and took something on. I had a bad night of sleep afterwards and Karl and I were drained, even the next day. We had a few tapping noises here, the chandelier started moving and we were drained like I said, apart from all the noise and upset around us. I saw a lot of horrible people in spirit with despair and anger during the ritual cleansing and this was linked to the house.

As far as I can see Terry has something very nasty attached to her house. It seems that Terry's mind is keeping the gate open and her mind is quite strong. I believe on the one part there is an earth elemental type spirit rather than your "normal" one. There is something not right with the aunt too. It is also related to the aunt; although she has physically left the house she is still attached in some way. I have asked the doorkeeper to close the doors and the elemental activity will diminish eventually, but the lady's fear (nervousness / apprehension) is not helping, and there is a woman in spirit around her too who is associated with the aunt, and she is really evil and is also causing these issues. Terry may say she is not nervous, but when the lights go out or she is on her own, there must be some apprehension. We also seem to have lower elementals that are attracted to the situation and the aunt's unconscious presence is not helping the situation too. Whatever her aunt did in the past, it was bad. She is not very nice from what I can pickup.

I believe we can tell Terry that it will diminish eventually, but more slowly than she might want. Any upsetting event or trauma will magnify the negativity around them and draw a reaction from the elementals. I can tell you that the energies around her are much diminished. But it seems there is a lot that she has not told us in relation to the family. I have been picking up on something that is even to the point of murder, at least one person has been murdered in the family and the intensity of ill will and bad feeling [gives the impression that] it is almost on the edge of being a curse. I believe that her son is easily influenced by the presences and this may explain some of the damage that is around. I definitely have a feeling of resentment, almost of an intrusion, into the son's life. I suggest that you state the following to her:

I went through the experiment and I connected with some presences in the house, I did draw most of the elements away and the rest should diminish as time goes on. I suggest that the lady in question and her son should say a ritual prayer every evening before they go to bed and imagine the house filling with light. Whilst there may be a residue of activity, eventually it will fade away. The worst of the darkness is gone. Please tell the lady that nothing can harm her if she puts out thoughts of peace and love to herself and the remaining elements in the house. Where there is love there is light, and the darkness cannot stand the light of love and understanding. All she has to do is ask her guardians and guides for help, and she will be helped. Oh, and by the way, I kept getting very clear image of The Virgin Mary.

The really strange part of all this was the reaction of Patrick's neighbours when the ritual began. I mentioned this to him and suggested that it might be likely that the 'elementals' that seem to be at the root of what is happening in Mexico may have had some influence on this. This would make sense, because if 'they' were aware of what was planned, and there is no reason to think differently, then they may have tried to make it as difficult as they could. It is as if they had flooded the location around the ritual with negativity, for do not forget that, as Patrick has already hinted at, they are fully aware of us and what we do even if we are not always aware of them. In effect, this relationship acts as a kind of 'two way street' where the multiple realities impinge upon one another, although it seems as if, due to their physical make up, the 'other side' is much more sensitive than we are. The best we can hope for is that they continue to regard us (the human race) as a minor nuisance and nothing more. There are some nasty entities out there that have no time for us and they continually seek to gain access to our reality.

Chapter 27
The Initial Results

All we could do now was wait to see what came back for Mexico, and when they arrived the results were not too encouraging, here is what came from Terry.

(T) We followed our instructions precisely, but I still hear the clicking near the windows and mirrors. When I arrived home this afternoon, I was welcomed by a rather large gouge in my armoire at the top of a staircase. I actually do not know what to expect. Was the door shut, the poltergeist banished and I should see and feel an immediate improvement, or is it more of a gradual reduction and then a final dissipation? After we blew out the candles, it followed me from room to room, clicking, but then things got kind of quiet. As I write, I am listening to intermittent clicks along the window next to the bamboo garden. Any ideas about what to expect next? Of course, I am extremely grateful for the time that you and the mediums have put into my rescue. Let me know what you/they think.

In the wake of the exorcism I had asked a series of questions regarding the way in which the damage was caused and whether it had ceased or was decreasing. I also asked some more pointed questions about her aunt. Previously I had deliberately refrained from doing this because I did not want to create any unnecessary unease. Although in retrospect perhaps this was not the best way to have dealt with the problem.

(T) The damage to the armoire was well before the exorcism. Anyway, I haven't noticed much new damage over the last couple of days but by the clicks, it is still very definitely around. Sometimes it doesn't make new damage. It makes prior damage worse. However, I do believe that the clicks are fewer and somewhat further apart. I have been praying and I have let the candles burn. I have the house cleaned twice a week to keep the greasy feel under control and there does seem to be less grime.

As for my aunt, I loved her dearly all of my life. She was the most generous, kind-hearted, patient person a child could ever hope to have had in his/her life. She was my mother's baby sister and they remained best friends until the day my mother died. Shortly afterwards, my aunt was diagnosed with Alzheimer's and after having presided over the death of her husband, sister, brother and near death of her only son, all within a few years back to back, I stepped in to take care of her.

She was physically and emotionally exhausted from trying to go to each and every one's rescue. The people whom she attended to worshipped her, as did I. So here we are. If I had to name a family member that I believed was involved in the occult, it by no means, would have been her. On another note, what exactly is an earthbound elemental? From the little I know, I did not think they were mean-spirited or malicious. Anyway, this is a small update until you and the medium can put it all together.

I explained the differences between elementals and other types of entity to Terry and asked about what had occurred in her home while the ritual was underway in London. What follows is a short Q&A session based on the above email message and it comprises my responses to the original text.

(T) *We followed our instructions precisely but I still hear the clicking near the windows and mirrors. When I arrived home this afternoon, I was welcomed by a rather large gouge in my armoire at the top of a staircase. I actually do not know what to expect.*

(B) *Was this before or after the exorcism, the time difference makes it a bit confusing.*

(T) *Was the door shut, the poltergeist banished and I should see and feel an immediate improvement or is it more of a gradual reduction and then a final dissipation?*

(B) *The medium phoned us just after 11pm last night and he is sure that the doorway was shut also that this 'entity' was an 'earthbound elemental' attracted by your aunt (what on earth WAS she into in her younger days?). As regards the presence of a statue of the Virgin Mary; he thought that was very relevant. There is quite a bit of information, but that will follow when he does a write up on what occurred. Oh and he recommends praying regularly for the time being at least, not from any religious aspect, but to keep out negative energy. He also felt that your son being quite young might also have been inadvertently 'feeding' it. He also mentioned that you and your son might have unknowingly been reflecting this energy off one another, always a possibility.*

(T) *After we blew out the candles, it followed me from room to room, clicking, but then things got kind of quiet. As I write, I am listening to intermittent clicks along the window next to the bamboo garden. Any ideas about what to expect next?*

(B) *I have to wait for another response from the medium and I have forwarded this email to him. IMO (for what it's worth) the effects should fade away, but the medium also suggested that in the short term your expectation might produce some effects too.*

(T) *Of course, I am extremely grateful for the time that you and the mediums have put into my rescue. Let me know what you/they think.*

(B) *You are welcome, but let's see what comes from the medium; I'll send it when I receive it.*

(T) *To be honest the house feels a lot more settled. The clicking sounds, while still present, are definitely fewer and farther apart and they are also beginning to sound more distant, if that makes sense. I have already contracted with someone to begin making repairs around the house and in general, my son and I are feeling a lot more upbeat. We reviewed what we learned from this experience and our world view is completely altered.*

Just because WE don't believe it, doesn't make it not true! We have always, to some extent, understood the medium's final comments. While I have read A Course in Miracles, I now have a better understanding of the true role of faith and love. Fear simply cannot be given a seat at the table. In any event, I sincerely thank you for your time and all your help. I will try to make very good use of all that I have learned. Better late than never. Thanks again and again.

Chapter 28
A Turn for the Worse

The follow-on from this was, to say the least, disheartening, because it was clear that either the entity had not left, or at best was taking its time about it. This is what arrived next:

From Terry

(T) Sorry to have to write again, but things have not gotten much better despite our renewed determination, prayers, candles and repairs. We have a stone mason working in the house making much needed repairs, especially in the kitchen, and this morning the marble counter that he re-built and shined to a stunning finish was badly chipped and pot-marked. The clicks near the windows and mirrors are still fewer and indeed do often sound further away, but the damage is relentless. Do you still think it is residual or is this problem more serious then we imagined? On another note, I appreciate that you and the medium have reserved your true opinions from me, as a little information is a dangerous thing to the un-initiated, but what are your real thoughts about the true nature of the problem?

This was, of course, a consideration that the mediums and I had discussed: i.e. what to tell Terry? The person who is suffering under this kind of 'attack' is in a poor mental state anyway without adding to their woes. So we had initially decided to play it safe, in that while we always told the truth there was no benefit for anyone by including any 'gory details'. The main reason for this was because, as Patrick previously indicated, Terry's state of mind might make matters worse if she was afraid or in some kind of turmoil; the negativity that this could cause might allow the entity to remain. Her feelings for her aunt were also clear enough, and she obviously cared for the old lady a great deal.

For that reason I replied as follows, it was clear that she had now sensed our initial reticence in revealing the extent of the infestation.

(B) 'The truth is that you are reporting what is occurring and I accept that, the nature of the events seems to be due to some invading entity, but I would not entirely rule out the effects of EH. Anyway, let me pass this on to the medium and we'll see what he thinks, don't worry, we'll get there. One thing that does puzzle me is that it does not seem to happen when anyone is present and observing, which is why I suggested some kind of surveillance.'

I should elaborate on my own feelings here. This does not, however, alter the fact that Patrick felt that the aunt may have been a contributing factor, do not forget that the trouble did not begin until her aunt arrived in her home. I had speculated on whether there might have been any friction between the cleaner and the aunt. I was also reminded of the conversation between Terry and her aunt when the old lady experienced a spell of lucidity; this was when Terry was told that her aunt had done some 'evil things' in the past.

Terry did not know what these 'evil things' referred to and unfortunately the aunt did not elaborate. Besides, it would depend on how her aunt thought, and the values she placed on various things. One man's (or indeed woman's) evil is another person's pleasure or even indifference. Another thing that struck me as odd (although quite typically of these events) was the observation that there were no 'attacks' when there was anyone present and as a result of this I suggested that she set up some kind of monitoring system.

Seeing the logic in this she initially agreed and tried to set up a closed circuit TV system monitored through a computer, however as we will see in her reply (below) it was not done. From what she said in the latest communication and despite Patrick's observation that this might take some time to settle out, it was apparent that there was still activity in the house. I was mindful that her mental state played an important part in finalising the ritual, and it was clear that she was still concerned so she may have been inadvertently encouraging the entity to remain. With this in mind, and after consulting Patrick and Karl, we decided to conduct another ritual, I suggested this to Terry and she replied as follows:

(T) 'I am thrilled to hear that the medium is willing to try again. Things, for a while, did actually get better and maybe this time we will succeed completely. As you have often said, resolution of these problems is not an exact science so trial and error is often necessary. Monday is fine at 10:00 pm (your time) and yes, I still have the tone.'

'I read about the electrical hypersensitivity thing again and I don't think that is applicable in my case at all. Most people with EH apparently are the only ones who hear the clicks. My son hears the clicks. I have had guests who have asked me what the clicks were. Unless we all have EH, I doubt that that can explain what is going on. Additionally, EH does not explain the ongoing damage nor does it explain the disappearing paint which; by the way, continues to disappear. As for the marble counter, the chips and pockmarks make it look almost rustic but after a while, if it continues the grout will widen, the stones will be formed into ugly shapes and it will begin to look weird rather like the stone work in my garden and in front of my house and on the wall in my living room.'

'We have a computer program which can monitor any area of the house we direct it to, but we decided against its use it for two reasons:

1. If we managed to actually see something it might increase our fear

2. We had already lost a computer and two printers so leaving a small appliance plugged in seemed risky. Having said that, we have not lost any small appliances recently so we can try to make a recording (triggered by movement) if you want us to. I still have the camera equipment etc. For your information, sometimes the damage does happen when I am present, but I do not realize that it is happening. Once I was working on my lap top and there was a lot of clicking in the room. When I got up to go to bed, I realized that there were weird markings (like stripes) on the floor tiles behind me that were not there before. Apparently I was right there when it happened. Other things similar to that have happened as well so I think it does happen when I am present but I am unaware that it is happening. Thanks for your willingness to try again. I really, really need to resolve this.'

'I am not sure if this will be helpful or not but when this experience first began nearly two years ago, around the time that my plants started to die we were living in what we often referred to as the 'dead zone'. Apart from the plants dying, nothing was blooming either. The spring passed without a single flower. Since my house is surrounded by plants and gardens, it was really odd when the spring came and went and we did not have a single flower. Moreover, the birds stopped chirping. The garden usually attracts lots of humming birds and we never saw one all that spring. When a stray bird would inadvertently stray onto our property it would take flight in a panic.'

Returning briefly to the strange syndrome of electrical hypersensitivity, I had suggested that the clicks might be due to an odd condition called 'microwave hearing', which can be caused by exposure to microwave radiation. The fluid in the inner ear is heated by the microwaves and expands slightly and this can cause the person so affected to hear a 'click'. It was part of the process of searching for alternative reasons for what was happening, and – therefore - a legitimate question, but the response from Terry and the additional information made this possibility increasingly unlikely. We made arrangements for another exorcism. However, just before the details were finalised this arrived:

(T) 'The attack against the marble in the kitchen has become so devastating that last night we covered the counter and the arched entrance to the kitchen with plastic bags. The immediate question is, "How on earth does THAT help/?" I am not sure, but as a rule when things are covered or put away, they seem to be safe. So we covered the marble and are hoping for the best. Everywhere in the house there is damage, including the outside areas and the roof. Several places on the roof have wet spots and that is really weird because I had the entire roof repaired last year. But the kitchen is a special place of concern to the entity.'

'Maybe something important to it used to be there or maybe it is because it is my personal favorite part of the house and I spend a lot of time there cooking for friends. Who knows? One other thing...I have a bedroom set with marble in the doors of the bureau and marble slabs on top of the furniture. It has all mostly been destroyed/severely damaged with nicks and dings. However, I have a large granite coffee table in my living room and while the entity has attacked the base of the table (which is wood) it has not touched the granite itself.'

'Also, there are now areas of the house that are starting to look scorched. By that I mean REALLY REALLY dry with a yellowish hue. Scorched? I know it sounds like I live in some huge country manor in the middle of a posh neighborhood. But I don't. It is an attached row house in the middle of a working class neighborhood. I just happen to have a lot of nice things and I plant gardens and trees everywhere I have ever lived. Let the medium know that if he would be willing to come, I would happily pay his fare and expenses. If we are unable to resolve this tomorrow, please ask if he might be amenable to this idea. I need help and aside from you gentlemen and the good graces of your wife, I am out of my depth and completely lost.'

Almost on the heels of this email, another one arrived:

(T) 'Oddly, the nicks and dings have become much larger. They are gashes and gouges now. They are especially noticeable because they are occurring in areas that I just had repaired. It is relentless. We are not afraid nor are we hostile or combative in the house, but nothing we do seems to work. Two nights ago, I saw it. At night it seems to hang out in the master bathroom. Usually I can hear it clicking away in there. I was laying across the bed and from my peripheral vision I saw the back of what appeared to be a tall man in something like a trench coat, but what I remember most of all was that he was wearing a pair of light colored boots. They were dirty but they stood out. In one of the emails, one of the mediums mentioned a pair of boots. Do you think we should try the DIY exorcism? Yikes!!! My friend (the former Catholic priest) might be able to help us. What do you think?'

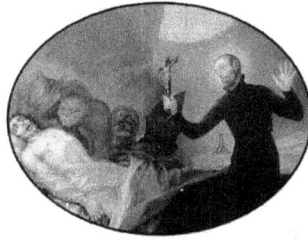

Chapter 29
Temporarily at a Loss

I contacted Patrick immediately, because judging from the way this was written the poor woman was becoming increasingly alarmed and depressed, just the kind of emotional hell that the invading entity might relish; this is why these beings are sometimes referred to as 'psychic vampires'. We arranged for the exorcism to be conducted the following day at the same local times as before. From what the mediums told me, the methodology would be identical to before and would be filmed as it progressed. We could only wait and see what would happen this time.

Both of the mediums had read these emails because I forwarded them as soon as they arrived, so they had seen the offer to pay for travel and accommodation costs should they decide to make the journey to Mexico. The offer was obviously attractive and genuine, but none of us were involved in this case to secure any form of reward. Besides, so far there was no real need to travel, especially as the 'battle' could be won remotely, because in the reality inhabited by this entity, distance and proximity were irrelevant. There was another constraint too, once any form of money or other reward is involved, especially from private individuals, then a certain expectation is created. This might be fine if that expectation is fulfilled, but if it is not then resentment soon enters the equation and for that reason we decided not to take up the offer.

Actually this matter raises some interesting points; if any medium, psychic or indeed paranormal investigator decided that it would be beneficial to travel to a location, especially if they were not specifically invited, then this would (or should) be at their own expense. On the other hand, if these parties were invited to attend an exorcism or similar phenomenon and it was some distance away, then the subject of expenses accompanied by receipts might be appropriate. This would be especially true if, for example, a TV programme intended for network transmission was being made concerning a specific case and the investigator/mediums were asked along as consultants. In that case a fee would be perfectly reasonable, besides, as a legitimate expense the budget for the show would (or should) make allowances for this.

Terry also makes mention of the priest performing his version of exorcism. This is reasonable and was something that we had not forgotten about. However, we decided to try another exorcism first, so after trying to set Terry's mind at rest this is exactly what we did. Just prior to it taking place, I received another (short) email from Mexico accompanied by more jpeg images. This time they were of strange discoloured patches on fresh plaster that had been applied inside her house. Terry had employed local contractors in an attempt at removing traces of the damage that had been caused by this unwelcome and malicious entity.

At first sight I was reminded on the strange 1971 case of the so called 'Belmez Faces' where strange images of human faces appeared on the concrete floor of a house in the village of Belmez de la Morelada in Jaen, Spain. The 'faces', which were - in the main - more like drawings and paintings rather than photographic images, began to appear from time to time. The occupants of the house, the Periera family, tried to remove the faces by repeated and vigorous scrubbing and cleaning, but they continued to appear. They have been the subject of considerable attention and, predictably, have been denounced as frauds and fakes, but the faces kept appearing. This is not to say that what appeared in Terry's house were faces, but the premise was the same. Bearing that in mind I suggested this possibility to Terry, and her reply was as follows:

> (T) *'It does not seem to be around right now, but I will try with yes/no questions as soon as I hear the clicks/taps again and see the light in the house go down. The low light circumstance seems to go with the clicks. Sometimes I can actually see the shadow move in. That is to say it seems like a cloud passing over the sun but it isn't. The room where it is will be somewhat darker and the rest of the house will have more light. In any event, I will try to communicate with it in the manner you suggest when next I have an opportunity.'*

> *'As for the faces of Belmez...who knows? My mind immediately went to defective cement but the color is so vivid and the places where the color is appearing were all done at different times with different materials. The master bathroom was just done last week with newly purchased cement and that wall has the largest image. Actually the faces don't sound so bad if they don't destroy anything. And turning the place into a tourist attraction might help me raise the cash to move! Got lemons? Make some lemonade!!'*

It was heartening to see that, if nothing else, she had not lost her sense of humour, something that is often vital in cases of this kind.

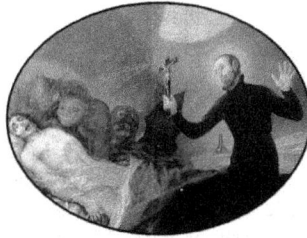

Chapter 30
The Second Exorcism, 20th September

Once again the date and time were set; we decided that given the time difference 10pm was still appropriate. There is no point setting out the ritual again since it was virtually identical to the first and once again it was filmed, but it is worth noting that this time there was no unwelcome din from the houses surrounding that of the mediums. When the recording was examined a little later there were no signs of the 'dark shapes' previously seen flitting around the séance room. Why should this be? Perhaps much of the impetus and venom had been drawn during the first attempt and what was still occurring in Mexico were 'aftershocks', almost like residual energies still attached to the fabric of the house. It was pretty much exactly what Patrick had said, i.e. this would take a little time to settle out and Terry's concerns and worries might have been adding to the situation.

We waited with mixed feelings to see what, if any, the response would be, and for a few days there was nothing, and on the basis that no news was good news, in the short term we were happy with that. When Terry did reply she was able to confirm that the symptoms continued to diminish, and the clicks etc., were much fainter and much fewer. The situation remained static for a few days, or so it seemed, because there were no further communications from her during the intervening period. Unfortunately this soon changed. I received a series of emails from her informing me, once again, that the phenomena seemed to be increasing in intensity and as it turned out, dare one say it, boldness! Before continuing, it is worth reiterating that throughout this ongoing project Patrick and Karl had repeatedly remarked that the unfortunate Terry might well be contributing to and exacerbating the problem by having it in her mind more or less continually.

The answers did not arrive until a full seven days later and they were, to say the least, ambiguous:

27th Sep

(T) 'Just a quick note to let you know that things are much better. The presence is still here and as evidence we continue to have small knicks and dings (especially along the corners of the walls) as well as dripping paint, but overall the damage is much, much less. There is some stone around the entrance to the front door which has been a focus of attention since the beginning and now the stone is being reshaped into very sharp points, but the damage to this area is not new.

First the spaces between each stone were widened, then the squiggly shapes around the edges and now the fine points. I do still hear a few clicks/taps each day (mostly in the early morning when I first get up around 5:00am) but the nights have been very quiet. Sometimes the noise would startle me right out of my sleep, but nothing like that has happened in a very long time. The house feels less heavy and dark and this is the longest that we have gone in more than 2 years without an aggressive return. We are OK and just keeping you posted. I keep hoping this will have a happy ending'

There were another few days with no contact then this arrived:

8th October

(T) 'Last week was awful. Paint was melting everywhere, but that was about it. No holes, no gouges and aside from the area around the front door, not much damage to the walls or stone. About three nights ago I was awakened by the sheets in my bed rustling. Since I was alone the noise awakened me immediately. I was kind of afraid and considering a run to my son's room, but being too lazy to get up, I fell back asleep and that seemed to have been that. I do believe the influence is fading, but not in a continual or gradual fade, but rather an ebb and flow type of fade. Does that make sense? We cleaned up the paint splashes this weekend and while the clicking/tapping continues it is also not constant like before. Sometimes it is a lot, but most often not. Also the copal incense seems to help. When I hear the clicking I burn either copal, frankincense or myrrh and the noises always stop unlike before when the incense had no effect. What do you think?'

Before continuing to the next, and rather more worrying email, we should pause to look at what is being said here. What did I think? That is a good question and in relation to what Terry says about the apparent reaction of this entity to the use of incense, in this case 'copal', is certainly interesting. Incense is a natural, traditional substance used for millennia in situations like this as it can reputedly either help to invoke, or dismiss, a 'spirit', and it is used in conventional religious ceremonies for precisely the same reason. The Catholic Church uses pleasant smelling incense during rituals associated with the Mass, chiefly during the ritual associated with Transubstantiation when, according to Church dogma, Christ in a very real sense is present on the altar. In this case, the incense contains such fragrant substances as myrrh, frankincense and resins like the aforementioned copal; I do not believe that other than in a 'New Age' sense Terry was aware of this particular use.

Frankincense is associated with the sun and also the male principle, while myrrh is associated with healing and the female principle. These attributions exactly define many ancient mystical and magickal traditions attached to the two sexes; man is the sun while woman is the caring and nurturing healer. Copal on the other hand is a generic title for a variety of granular resins that occur in a range of colours and are used for purification and cleansing the spirit, and also various ritual items used during ceremonies.

As far as the Church is concerned, the smoke from the incense is ostensibly used as a visual sign that the prayers of the faithful are being carried up to heaven. Of course, its more important use, and the one not quite so well acknowledged, involves cleansing the area of evil spirits and other undesirable entities, which is the aspect of its use that Terry was invoking. The ritual use of incense, which long predates its Christian function, seems to stem from the ceremonies of the ancient Egyptians, and it was also widely used in China and throughout Southeast Asia.

We also find that overtly magickal practises also use various incenses for a number of reasons, some positive and other less so. Satanic groups use various substances, but mainly 'patchouli', also and perhaps significantly called *'graveyard dust'*, to invoke a variety of demons for use in clairvoyance, healing and if necessary to throw a curse. Once again the use of incense is intended to signify that something remarkable or special is about to take place, a time when 'change' can occur. Incense is also utilised in pagan and Wiccan settings where it is employed for similar, but less threatening, purposes and the 'energy' contained in the fragrance of the incense can be used to enhance the magick being performed. Once again, it is arguable that what Terry is doing here amounts to a magickal cleansing. The Wiccan interpretation of incense usage comes from the assumption that the material comprising the incense combines the four earthly elements of fire (to burn it), water (produced while it burns) air (which carries the fragrance) and earth (in which constituents grow), so it fits snugly into their magickal philosophy.

Chapter 31
Staying Positive

Throughout the duration of this strange series of events, both the mediums and I had tried to keep Terry thinking positively as this is one real advantage. Although much of what had been said (and I cannot overstate this) was anodyne in nature, there was still a clear message which was not to give up. An example of these exchanges is neatly summed up, and encapsulated in this message on October 9th from Patrick and Karl; we had to keep repeating that the process might take some time and that she might be unwittingly contributing to the situation.

(K&P) 'The barrier has been put up but it will take time to fully close. I did another ritual last night in a different location probably just before or about the same time she sent the email. It's interesting how she linked the activity around the Aunt with the activity in the house. There was a lot of nastiness associated with the Aunt and is still there. I don't think you know the full truth about the family situation there. She should confront the situation head on. Not accepting the poltergeist activity or damage. By standing up to it she can stop things happening. The truth of it is that her mind is empowering the situation. If she disregards the paranormal activity, or at least disempowers it by literally telling it that I am taking your power away, then it will be reduced.'

The reply was almost by return and the contents were mixed:

10th October

(T) 'Please let Patrick know that I am grateful. Last night again something very weird happened. During the late night or early morning it slipped into my bed again. I sort of woke up but thought that it was my son (early on he used to get frightened and come into my room). So I moved over without really thinking. When I asked him about it this morning he said that it was not him. YIKES!!!! Something happened on that side of the bed, because when I woke up there were a few large drops of water on the floor right next to the bed (absolutely no place water could have come from) and two new sizable dings on the night stand next to my bed.'

'I am thinking that I might be going through the poltergeist stages because the water appearing in strange places is sort of where it all began. The damage to the furniture and the water was at the very beginning. Also, yesterday by happenstance I ran into the woman who runs the nursing home where my Aunt is. She told me that my aunt has been unusually aggressive of late and actually bit her on the hand the day before. Could these things be related? I continue to send you the details (at least as I understand them) because something might contain an important clue that might help the situation to resolve. On a more positive note (I think) the smudges and slashes on the walls are no longer scarlet colored or black. They are now grey and quite easy to remove unlike the earlier ones.'

Strange indeed. The entity is evidently now attempting a degree of intimacy by getting into bed with Terry. This cannot be a reassuring sign and there are the small pools of water appearing, as mentioned earlier the appearance of small pools of water is, of course, a common feature of supposed poltergeist manifestations. The fact that her aunt displayed some aggression may not necessarily be relevant here since people with a range of neurological conditions (like Alzheimer's) frequently display uncharacteristic reactions and responses, although Patrick's initial impressions regarding the old lady may have more than a little justification. As it turned out there was no internet traffic of any kind for some weeks and it looked as if the situation was resolving itself nicely. However our relief was short lived when things took a turn for the worse again when this message arrived on the 11th of December:

'I have a couple of things to share with you which may be of interest to you and your research. I think that I have mentioned in a previous email that I have a black granite table in my living room which has not been scarred, dented or scratched in any way. All other stone in the house has pretty much been destroyed. In the meantime, I began the restoration/replacement of the arches and counter in my kitchen and initially, I covered the new work with black plastic bags to protect it and it went untouched. Then I decided to remove the black plastic bags and re-cover the new arches with a clear plastic so the house would be a bit more cheerful. Overnight, the kitchen counter was destroyed and the stonework on the arches was being cut into ever smaller pieces. The whole thing started over again. The following day I recovered everything with the black plastic bags and the damage has stopped. Visual component? Energy absorption?' 'Then suddenly the house seemed very tranquil for several days and shortly afterward I was told that my aunt had lapsed into a deep sleep and had to be rushed to the hospital. Since she has been in the hospital (without hope of recovering) the house has been quiet and click/tap free. Of course I attend to her at the hospital everyday and yesterday while using the bathroom in her room, I noticed the same type of damage behind the bathroom door that is behind all the bathroom doors in my house. The damage is very distinct with the same type of cut edges. What do you think of all this? Any advice?'

I replied that we could only wait and see, but once again there was a hiatus and no communications were received from Terry, until sometime later this arrived.

Chapter 32
From Terry 11th Jan 2011

'Hi Brian.

Hope you had a pleasant Christmas and are looking forward to a great New Year! Just a quick email to bring you up to date and ask your opinion on events. My aunt died 5 days ago. While she was in decline things got very quiet in the house and while there was still a small amount of damage, the direction seemed clear. Then she died and the following three days were horrible. There were VERY loud clicks on the first day. So much so that a house guest became frightened and was relieved to leave for the US the following day. The grime/greasy feel of the house returned and the grout in the stone work began to disappear leaving dozens of holes. There were also holes punched directly into the stone. Additionally, the stone called Cantera (a type of limestone, I believe) suddenly had odd black and grey discolorations all over it. Then things got quiet again yesterday and the house seemed to be much brighter.'

'By that I mean the lower level of the house had become a bit gloomy. The natural light seemed to enter less and less and on cloudy days it was outright depressing. I had assumed that the black plastic bags draped over everything were absorbing the light and had become part of the problem, but maybe not. Anyway, the light has returned to all three floors despite the black bags. But, the story is not yet over. I can still hear intermittent clicking and this morning there were black slashes on the floors downstairs and the walls upstairs despite the light returning to the house. I think I mentioned to you that at times the house would grow dim, kind of like clouds passing in front of the sun. '

'Then one day it just stayed that way, but yesterday the light returned. Does any of this sound familiar to you? What do you think? And finally, I was able to answer the question of whether or not to attempt a move to a different house. The answer is NO. I spent Christmas with friends and family at my beach house and after a couple of days I began to see very familiar damage on the furniture there as well. Whatever it is, travels with us.'

I replied to Terry on the same day:

(B) 'Hello Terry,

I will of course pass all this along to Patrick; about the beach house...were your friends and family aware of any of the phenomena and if so what did they say? The events you describe all seem inextricably interlinked: the fading light, the damage etc. Please bear in mind what Patrick has said about what he senses around your son though as this could well be providing an additional point of contact. However from what you say I get the impression that it may well all slowly dissipate with the passing of your aunt. I wish we could make this happen more quickly but we cannot. All I can do is suggest that you keep voicing the rejections and denials of whatever it is. As I said right at the start, this will take time but it WILL go.'

I forwarded all of this on to Patrick, and Karl and Patrick asked me to request a photograph of the aunt and I forwarded it to Patrick as soon as it arrived, his response is as follows...

From Patrick

(P) Brian,

'There appears to be several grounded entities attached to the Aunt which are also feeding off the son who also has a strong psychic ability and is a focus. They seem to be quite revengeful for some reason; something interrelated to the Aunts past life and at the moment she is neither on the earth nor in spirit but somewhere in between. And this is creating the conditions for the destruction at the moment. But once again, rejection and disempowerment of the entities is the answer. The power of the will is the strongest weapon at their disposal. Just as I tried to close the door before, I will try to do again. This will come to an end and the doors will close. They must have faith and know that there is a power of good that they can tap into that which will help them if they ask for the help and this is my advice Brian. I should add that what is written here is a slightly more anodyne version because the original was considerably more forceful and quite alarming; but the meaning is identical.'

I forwarded this to Terry hoping that it would provide some sort of relief; however the response was not at all reassuring and seemed to have little or no relevance to the message, although given what had occurred, it is small wonder.

From Terry 12th January

(T)'Brian,

About two days ago my bottom teeth felt strange. Kind of rough, but I did not pay it much attention. Then my bottom row of teeth began to really hurt as in extremely sensitive to both hot and cold. When I looked closely in the mirror I realized that my bottom row of teeth had been shaved and on one of my eye teeth, the point had been shaved away. When I mentioned the event to my son, he showed me where his teeth have small nicks and dings on his two large front teeth.

My situation is painful and I have to go to the dentist to see what can be done. When I first realized what was happening I had high anxiety. I am over it now but what do you think? Oh what in the world can we do? This destructive and mean entity may have entered through my aunt but it seems to be very independent of her now nor does it seem to be dissipating. The damage in the house does seem to be less and the light is better but this thing with our teeth is very disconcerting. Maybe I will need to pay Patrick's way after all. My son is becoming frightened'.

I immediately replied trying to give some kind of reassurance and urging the poor woman to seek some kind of spiritual reassurance, but this was nigh on impossible. However, I did try to remain upbeat about it all, and Terry's reply was as follows.

From Terry 12ᵗʰ January (again)

'I did talk to someone in the archdiocese here, but they try not to acknowledge or accept exorcism except in extreme cases. They explained that they would only perform one if an actual person were showing very serious signs of demonic possession indicated by things way more extreme than what has been going on here. Extreme, I imagine, like everything else, is in the eye of the assessor. Moreover, by the time they get approval from the Vatican, we will have all died of natural causes. I am probably not going to get much help from the church. Honestly, for the first time I am REALLY worried.'

From this latest communication it was only too clear that in addition to reiterating the intransigence of the Roman Catholic Church when we first began dealing with this problem, things were going from bad to worse. This was beyond what had seemed like a 'last fling' from the entity. Again I tried to reassure her (there was little else I could do) saying that much of what she said was true and what the Church considered as 'demonic possession' varied, but for the most part tended to follow a set pattern. I suggested trying Google because there was an absolute goldmine of valid and useful information on the subject there. The Church does set strict rules by which they operate. However, the permission does not come from the Vatican, but from the local bishop. This is what I sent:

(B) 'The Catholic Church is not the only organisation that conducts exorcisms either, remember what I told you about Pentecostal and other charismatic groups? What about 'deliverance ministry'? That's worth a try although this can be, to say the least, very theatrical. There is still also the possibility of using the services of a shaman because they are every bit as good and effective, in Mexico making contact with one should not be too difficult. Try to contact one of these groups, but steer clear of any self-proclaimed 'ghostbusters' as they can be worse than useless plus many of them have their own agenda. This is easy for us to say, but PLEASE try not to worry and KEEP DENYING IT and giving it any encouragement of any kind...get angry at it, get mad, yell at it, tell it to GET OUT. But most importantly you MUST BELIEVE that this will work. If the worst comes to the worst there is always the RR. BTW, I'm still awaiting word back from Patrick, he may be away from home at present.'

From Terry
14th January

(T) 'As luck would have it, I was in a class this weekend with a very good friend. Out of desperation I spoke to him about my problem. As it turns out, he knows a Jesuit priest who is an exorcist and is on the list of official exorcists of the Catholic Church. He is in his eighties and has probably forgotten more than I will ever know Anyway, my friend will put me in touch with him next week and we will see what happens. I will definitely keep you posted!'

My reply was immediate:

(B) That's absolutely great, things have a habit of sorting themselves out one way or another. Just synchronicity? Nah, there has to be something much deeper than that, I look forward to hearing what happens, besides, the old priest will probably know other exorcists which can't be bad. I will of course pass all this along to Patrick. About the beach house...were your friends and family aware of any of the phenomena and if so what did they say?

The events you describe all seem inextricably interlinked: the fading light, the damage etc. Please bear in mind what Patrick has said about what he senses around your son though as this could well be providing an additional point of contact. However from what you say I get the impression that it may well all slowly dissipate with the passing of your aunt. I wish we could make this happen more quickly but we cannot. All I can do is suggest that you keep voicing the rejections and denials of whatever it is. As I said right at the start, this will take time but it WILL go.'

The next message arrived many months later.

Chapter 33
Terry 23rd August 2011

(T) Hi Brian,

I hope this communication finds you and your family well. I have not written in quite some time because I have been so frustrated. I am no longer asking for help but rather updating you for the purpose of the book project and your research. As you will recall my aunt died in December and at first the paranormal events continued without missing a beat and then things got real quiet.

I think I might have written to you at that time to say that a calm had settled over our lives and things felt peaceful. But sadly, not long after that the whole thing started again. I began to hear the clicks and the damage resumed on the stone etc. We have it all covered in black again. The black granite table in the living room remains untouched but the black wrought iron hand rails along the staircase now have cuts and holes and is looking like part of it is melting.

The really weird thing that happened is that every single piece of art in the house has been altered. That is to say that ADDITIONS have been made. For example, I have an oil painting of two boys sitting on a dock watching the water and now the surrounding sea has a lot of red in it (the colour on my roof) and other alterations. I have another foil painting that is framed under glass, of a vase with several roses. One morning I woke to find that a total of six new roses (ugly roses of course) had been added to the picture. And so on for every picture in the house.

At the beach house I have an abstract piece of art around which a series of white boxes have been drawn. The whole thing is just too weird. In the meantime, I bought a chocolate Labrador retriever. Since my son is never home, I decided to get a replacement. A dog is probably a step up from another husband, but I digress...Anyway, when the dog first arrived (he was 5 months old at the time) he seemed to sense the presence of something, but did not seem alarmed. He sort of ran after it to the window in my room where most of the clicks come from and then he settled down and went to sleep.

The dog has not particularly reacted to the situation...that is until today. I was in my office working and usually he just sleeps in the corner while I do whatever I am doing. The dog has a very calm disposition and is usually very gentle. But today, each time he would enter my office he would go berserk barking and growling. Frankly, up until today I had never even heard the dog growl. Anyway, I had to lock him in the kennel before he calmed down. Four years is a very long time for this kind of event, isn't it? I am starting to crack!

I thought it best to send this latest email to Patrick who had performed the first exorcism (or battle depending on how you look at it),and this is his reply.

Reply from Patrick

(P) 'Well Brian,

There are a few interesting points with this and I think that she is still holding on to this negative energy and causing a lot of the problems herself. I think there is another grounded spirit involved, and this time it is not the Aunt...but it is, one of the spirits that was using the resentment and the frustration of both the son, and Terry herself.

The fact that Terry feels guilty about the Aunt, and also the fact that her relationship with her son has not improved, i.e. the way it was before she brought the Aunt in, this is adding to the negative energies around her. It really is a case that you can exercise the spirit or negative energies around her, but ultimately she has to stop opening the door and letting them in again.

I'll say this, when I asked the question I was told that she does have a tangible presence there. There is a very strong negative presence. I am also being told that it's not just one but two or three spirits associated with the house, and the area. One is an ex-soldier. There are two or three people either buried in the grounds of the house or directly beneath it, and the negative emotional resonance created by the presence of the Aunt when she was in limbo between life and the after world, opened up these vibrations in the house. There was a strong 'tap' from spirit here in response to this answer. [*Note, Patrick communicates directly with whatever external energy surrounds us, he chooses to refer to it as 'spirit'. It responds to his questions in various ways] And although the presence of the Aunt is no longer there, the negative energy and spirit entities that she empowered are now in both Terry's aura and also the sons.

They are feeding off of the interplay of negativity between the two of them. This lady has a very powerful psychic energy, but she doesn't know how to control it and is frankly quite terrified by it. The son also has a great deal of energy but I get a very negative energy field around him. There is a lot that is quite unpleasant in his aura.

As I say, we can close the door and I am willing to try again, but ultimately as in all cases of possession, or obsession from the spirit world, they can only stay if they are allowed access in the first place. Whilst I can slam the door, if the darker entities keeps getting their fingers caught in it, each time they come back, the negativity or the bad energy and fear created will just empower them even more.

She herself must understand that she has the power to get rid of these entities, but she has to believe in it. Hence it is like a form of exorcism, calming the mind and giving a positive attitude. Thoughts are living things and can be used positively or negatively, so she has to re-programme herself.

As you know Brian most negative spirits are a bit like the wizard in the "Wizard of Oz" the only thing that empowers them is the fear and negativity of the individuals involved. I will of course try to help in any way I can, but you must have drawn similar conclusions yourself'

I sent this comprehensive report to Terry pretty much 'as is' because it was probably better all round that she be made aware of Patrick's impressions.

25th August 2011 Terry's response

(T) Brian,

I have taken several days to think about what is written here and there are some things that I agree with wholeheartedly and others that I feel are not true at all. Also, I recognize that because I do not feel that something is true doesn't mean it isn't. This problem is sort of like figuring out a puzzle. I just need to find the pieces that fit. Read my response below. In any event, convey my great appreciation to Patrick for hanging in there with me.

Well, after having spoken with my son about all that Patrick said as well as my responses to you, he flat out declared me delusional! He said that I felt VERY guilty about having taken our aunt from her beloved home in Arizona. In fact, he said that I used to cry frequently and wonder out loud about what else I might have done that might have made her happier. Forget about the, "I never felt guilty" part.

My son also said that, of course, I am negative and continue to empower the entity. He said that I am fairly obsessive about checking the house for new damage on a daily basis and he finds the behaviour, aside from being somewhat compulsive, rather dark and negative. So let's forget about the, "I don't feel negative" part too. Denial is more than just a river in Egypt! Happily, he said that the rest of my statements were true from his point of view as well. Like I always say, "Just because you don't believe it, doesn't make it not true". I am working on my attitude as I write.

28th August 2011

'Brian,

Well, as a matter of fact, things **ARE** different. The entity is still here and still making those clicking sounds but it has basically stopped damaging things beyond repair. I haven't seen any serious new damage for the past couple of weeks. There are a few new paint splatters but they are small and easy to remove. Also, I am a teacher and my first class is at 7:00 a.m. One morning I over-slept and an extra loud click woke me up. Another night I fell asleep in the family room watching TV and when I awakened around 2:00 am, the TV as well as the cable box were both turned off. What was funny about it was that the lights were still on so it clearly wasn't a power outage. Also, the feel around the house is a lot less intimidating. The woman who cleans the house has also commented that she is finding fewer and fewer things that have been damaged, thereby confirming my perception.'

'I personally, have been paying less and less attention to the general phenomenon and taking Patrick's advice very seriously, and my son barely noticed anything anyway so we have emotionally moved on. The entity can no longer feed from my energy. The intensity just isn't there anymore. Just as Patrick said of the Wizard of Oz, I have seen the man behind the curtain and he just wasn't as scary as I thought! Let me know what's happening on your end. Regards to Ann because I am aware that she is a quiet river running in the background.'

I should say that Terry makes a good point here, because although rarely mentioned, my wife, Ann, did in fact have input into this case and her opinions were invariably right. I have no real way of knowing this, but based on past experience, it does seem that Ann has an instinctive 'feel' for cases of this kind. Perhaps it is a latent psychic ability, or perhaps it is sheer pragmatism and common sense; either way it has paid me dividends more than once to heed her advice.

October 4th 2011. An end at last?

(T) 'Hi Brian,

Just a quick update for you. Things have quieted down. By "quiet down", the number of clicks I hear throughout the house has diminished and while there continues to be damage, it is not on the grand scale of earlier times. Unfortunately all of my art work has been destroyed and either adding or erasing things from the canvas seems to be its new preoccupation along with melting parts of the wrought iron handrails throughout the house. I used to obsess about the art, but I am over it. Also I have a large copper kettle in which I store small blankets etc. and big dark blotches are now on the kettle. I haven't bothered to check to see if the stains can be removed, but I would doubt it. Part of it looks like a burn of some sort and part of it looks like acid was somehow dripped on it. Just plain weird.

Something else unusual is also happening in the area where I live. While walking my dog, I have been noticing for quite some time now that there are white paint splatters on houses that are not painted white. In fact, there is oddly splattered white paint on a great many of the houses and gates. In part, this is what I began to initially notice happening in my own home. Everything began to look as if it had been painted carelessly but I am, at the heart of it, very meticulous and would have never allowed the painters to leave such an unsightly mess. While hard to explain, the splatters have a pattern which I am now expert at detecting. I also frequently catch the smell of copal burning in my neighbours' houses. The whole thing is really weird.

Sometimes my dog freaks out and chases "something" around the house while barking wildly. It actually doesn't happen all that often (maybe once a week), but when it does happen it is very disconcerting. Let me know what you think of the "neighbourhood" effect. Should I continue to burn the copal? Should I consider a DIY exorcism? Or just focus elsewhere like I have been doing? '

I replied to Terry (the last communication as it happens) to the effect that she should continue doing whatever seemed to work best and to remain upbeat, because given time it would all pass. And there the matter rests, and as far as I know she is still dealing with the matter on a day to day basis and it is clear that she is doing her best, but sometimes these matters cannot be dealt with easily and have no quick or easy ending.

There is no hard and fast conclusion to be drawn for what occurred, although it all helps as an added reference point to add to my own personal database of experience. Despite the fact that in almost all of the cases I have been involved with there has been a 'happy ending' of some kind and the invading entity was removed or, even better 'sent into the light', that is not always the case. We should understand that because these entities are not human they do not necessarily have to behave or react in predictable ways; although in many cases mentally ill human beings are similarly unpredictable (and extremely dangerous). In this, we seem to return to the link between mental illness and claims of possession. This seems to resonate with the cases described in the first part of the book; some responded quickly, some responded eventually and some never did, so it is clear that the scenario does not change, only the era and how the phenomenon is dealt with.

The downside of it, if one can call it a downside, is that as times and perceptions change so does how these entities are regarded. It is true that some unfortunate people have profound psychiatric issues requiring medical intervention to protect both them and the general public. In addition, (and unfortunately) there are unscrupulous religious schisms that are hell-bent on convincing the doubtful that they are possessed when they are not. Yet there is always the nagging doubt and suspicion that perhaps among them there are a few individuals genuinely possessed by some demonic or evil spirit.

There is little that can be done about it, and in the case of those who follow the medical route perhaps the medication they are prescribed does bring a measure of relief. Of those who are not possessed, but are pressured into thinking they are, well, we can only hope that they are not permanently scarred by the process. Those who are possessed and able to make contact with other ways of assessing and dealing with the matter, the one thing to take heart from is that in the majority of cases they can, and do, respond to a determined effort to remove the invading presence.

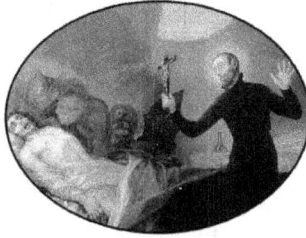

Chapter 34

Scratches!
The account of a demonic attack and its aftermath

As well as having a homemade exorcism carried out on me, I have also taken part in what are effectively exorcisms. This chapter describes a case of apparent possession I attended with 'John' the exorcist who carried out the exorcism on me a few months earlier. It is the account of a series of violent attacks on a 37-year-old man by an invisible assailant. The reality or otherwise of poltergeists and/or 'evil spirits' and the effect they have on the lives of the ordinary people they affect is difficult to gauge, but in this instance the weals and lesions inflicted on the victim were deep, painful, and very genuine.

The recipient of the unwelcome and terrifying attacks is in every sense of the word a normal family man. He is Andy Scott (pseudonym), a friendly and outgoing businessman who is married, has children, a mortgage and to all intents and purposes is like everyone else in his community. What is described here is another example of the close similarities between poltergeists and possession. The last thing Andy ever expected or considered was the intrusion of an invisible, malignant and violent entity into his life, and for a short while he was 'possessed', or, as it is sometimes described, 'overshadowed'. However, for several months in 2002 this is exactly what happened when he became the focus of a series of terrifying encounters with a particularly nasty and persistent spirit. Perhaps significantly the man who was the focus of the attacks was no stranger to paranormal happenings and had a history of supernatural encounters. Regrettably, since this was written 'Andy' has unfortunately passed over.

There was no apparent cause, pattern or precursor to the attacks that left him with dozens of deep, bloody scratches covering his back and arms. He would feel a sudden, sharp, burning sensation, which was quickly followed by the appearance of the wounds. I had the opportunity to examine and photograph some of these wounds, and those, especially on his back, were equidistant parallel lines and looked as if they had been inflicted by a clawed hand, raking its sharp nails over the skin. Both his arms were covered in scratches and there was a particularly deep gouge on his left bicep. This was particularly noticeable because of a tattoo, and the scratch was so deep that the ink comprising the image could be seen as coloured layers in the skin. The gouges on his right forearm appeared to be random and one group took the form of the letter 'Z', although this may have been coincidental.

By way of corroboration, at the onset of one attack Andy had just finished making a 'phone call while his brother-in-law stood beside him, when suddenly he felt the (by now) familiar burning sensation on his back. He quickly pulled off his 'T'-shirt and his brother-in-law watched in fascinated horror as the scratches appeared right in front of his eyes. Not surprisingly, both men were shocked and a little afraid, but neither was sure how to deal with the situation. There are no obvious personality profiles to identify people who become the recipient of poltergeist, if that is what it was, visitations, but traditionally there are reasons for manifestations of this kind.

Accepted wisdom suggests that, as discussed earlier, the entity 'feeds' on negative emanations from the victim, or, alternatively, is the unintentional by product of hormonally charged pubescent or 'troubled' children, usually but not exclusively female. It has also been established that the unwitting victim (or victims) of the attacks are not necessarily those creating or attracting the manifestation, but nevertheless become the focus. There is no good or obvious reason for this, but it is one commonly reported feature of the syndrome.

Previous encounters

During the course of a taped interview, some of the responses to the questions asked suggested that the cause of the attacks might not be due to Andy, but may have unintentionally been created by his wife who was experiencing some health problems at the time, and that may have served as the catalyst for the manifestations. It is also interesting, and possibly relevant, that Andy had both an apparent history of psychic encounters and an acceptance of paranormal events. During his occupancy of another business premises close to his present location he also reported a series of odd happenings. While there was nothing as remotely alarming as his current experiences, nonetheless he was certain that there was a 'presence' in the building.

The 'presence' had caused a number of small but unsettling incidents, including hiding small items and opening doors. Andy told me of the manifestations, and I became involved and when I interviewed him regarding these occurrences I unearthed a few fascinating and possible relevant details. Among the incidents, I found two that seemed to tie into the way in which electrical items can act in circumstances where paranormal events occur. There were two occurrences involving electrical equipment when a set of traffic direction indicators fitted to a bicycle began flashing on and off, the selector switch did not move, and a fluorescent light fitting on the premises switched on and off; the switch, which was in good condition, did not move.

There was only one incident that might be construed as alarming when a door securely held in place by toggles literally flew out of the frame and crashed to the floor, yet the toggles, which were still in the 'closed' position, were not damaged. While not in themselves conclusive, incidents like these are a common factor found when investigating claims of the paranormal. The incidents involving the traffic direction indicators and the light fitting tend to indicate the possibility of an EM element in the phenomena and this is also borne out by other reported instances where anomalous electrical equipment operation and/or failure is frequently reported.

I can vouch for this having witnessed the phenomenon during previous investigations, which included the spontaneous discharge of two fully charged camcorder batteries during an (apparently successful) attempt at 'channelling' an ET entity. The batteries had never malfunctioned prior to this occasion, and after subsequent re-charging functioned quite normally. In this instance, we concluded that the electrical energy stored in the batteries might have, in some manner, facilitated the session and allowed the 'entity' to communicate via the medium.

Following the interview, and in view of what Andy had to say, I invited two mediums to evaluate the situation. According to them, the presence was that of an elderly man who had become attached to the building and was there purely because he enjoyed the company. Andy even left a small chair for him in an area indicated by the medium and strange as it might seem, from then on there were no more bizarre events in the shop. Since the new outbreak of psychic activity was considerably more alarming and involved his family, Andy decided to request the services of two mediums to help eliminate the problem.

Although he had told me about the events, it was not until after he had contacted the mediums, both of whom were unknown to me. And unfortunately they refused to allow me to observe them as they carried out their rituals. They also asked Andy and his family to leave the house before they began, but he did observe one rather incongruous thing; one of them used a magnetometer. To use such a measuring device seems at odds with the methods traditionally employed by mediums and psychics as they operate, however equipment like this is part and parcel of a field investigators' test equipment.

It is designed to locate the presence of ambient and/or anomalous magnetic fields which may indicate the possibility of paranormal events occurring. Again this is by no means conclusive, but mounting evidence suggests that the two events may indeed be linked by some as yet unknown process. The meter used by the mediums indicated the presence of such a magnetic field in a corner of the living room in Andy's home, which, after he and his family returned, disappeared, and - more importantly - the poltergeist attacks also stopped.

Although unable to witness at first hand the events taking place in his house, I was able to photograph the marks and scars on his body. Likewise, while on this occasion I could not observe the mediums as they worked, thankfully the results appear satisfactory, but this is not the end of the story. In the weeks immediately following the events in his house, I arranged for 'John', the practitioner of Sufi mystical techniques - who we encountered at the beginning of the book - to carry out a cleansing ritual on Andy, which seemed to have a beneficial effect on him. I was able to observe the ritual as it took place and it appeared to be exactly the same as the one that John performed on me a few months earlier. However, unlike my own experience Andy did not collapse after the ritual was completed.

In the intervening months the attacks ceased, and there was peace in his house, but recently another series of incidents has begun. Andy's wife reports that she has been touched on the shoulder and hair by an unseen hand and she has heard noises and a voice calling her name when alone in the house. I followed this development with considerable interest, but fortunately the new incidents stopped as quickly as they had begun and have not returned, and again this is quite typical of these short term 'possessions'.

Chapter 35
Deliver them from Evil

The following case proved to be an exceptionally harrowing and moving experience for all concerned, and it was also an example proving that exorcisms (or cleansings) can occasionally be genuinely alarming affairs. Through the agency of the mediums involved this was, at the time, the closest I had come to a face-to-face encounter with the negative energy created by the entity involved. There was also a short example of what could be described as a poltergeist manifestation, something that is not uncommon in exorcisms. The ritual of exorcism used did not involve the all traditional tools of bell, book and candle, although one other traditional element (salt and water) was involved. Everything, although relatively low key, still managed to produce tangible results, and as far as we know all is still well with the people involved. Their names have been changed at their request; this is their story.

I was contacted in the January of 1999 by Mary Thompson (pseudonym) in respect of a neighbour, Jane Crosbie, (pseudonym), who was experiencing odd and unsettling happenings within her home. These took various forms including dull, heavy, dragging noises like slow deliberate footsteps emanating from her bedroom. It was a regular occurrence for Jane to arrive home to find both the television and gas fire turned on. Since Jane (who has been separated from her husband for around seventeen years) lived with her son (aged twenty) and had sole possession of all the house keys, this was extremely unnerving. I should add that when this was happening her son was not in the house either. Her neighbours had noticed that her bedroom curtains opened and closed apparently of their own volition, again when she was not at home. This, coupled to apparent physical attacks on her son by some invisible entity, had proved to be the last straw.

She mentioned the bizarre and unsettling phenomena to her friend Mary who offered to keep her company, and as a result of this Mary also experienced some of the phenomena at first hand. This took the form of deliberate thudding footsteps in the front hall moving from the front door to the kitchen. The footsteps were so heavy that the living room door vibrated on its hinges, but when they both looked into the hall, it was empty. Following this manifestation Mary asked Jane if she would like some help dealing with these problems. By this time she was understandably nervous and upset so she agreed. Following the report, I visited Jane at her home in a quiet, unremarkable street on an estate in a Stirlingshire village. I arrived to find four people in the house, Jane, her friend Mary and two other people one of whom was Mary's daughter; Jane told us her story.

She and her two children, who at the time were still young and living with her, had occupied the house for around seven and a half years and odd happenings had occurred since they first moved in. At first they were quite minor and she did not attribute them to any form of supernatural agency, but gradually they increased both in frequency and severity. At first they were fairly mild; footsteps, creaking boards, that type of thing. Jane, being a practical level-headed person, had attributed them to the normal sounds that a house produces due to natural expansion and contraction, drafts and noises from the neighbouring houses etc. However, her pragmatism was tested to the limit when she returned home from a short break to once again find her TV and gas fire on, (her son had been with her). She was also regularly awakened during the night by noises in her bedroom, and had the impression there was a presence in the room with her.

One night shortly after this, when she was about to get into bed, she drew the sheets back to discover that the mattress was soaking wet. This, as you will imagine, did nothing to improve her state of mind, but she dried the mattress as best she could, although not surprisingly did not sleep at all that night. Jane then recounted that the following night her son was awakened by the sensation of someone (or something) breathing on his face: this was not the first time it had happened. This type of incident had been happening on and off since he was three years old in other accommodation in which they had lived. During the night he would come into her bedroom telling of '*the big man*' in his room and ask her to make him go away.

At the time Jane attributed this to the fantasies all children experience and other than humouring him did not attribute anything unusual to it. However, in retrospect this may well have been another example of the 'invisible friends' syndrome, a concept that may originate in the fact that the brains of young children operate naturally in the 'alpha state'. The alpha state, which is recognised as a brain frequency of between 8 - 12 Hz, is presumed to be a common factor when sightings of ghosts and other psychic events occur. There is also some evidence that the slightly lower theta frequencies of around 5 - 8 Hz may produce similar phenomena.

As she spoke, I felt that I could recognise a familiar pattern beginning to emerge; this was reinforced when Jane told me of the recent apparent physical attacks on her son. These started with him being startled by a sharp pain on the instep of his foot as if he had been burned. He was sitting watching TV with his mother when the sharp pain caused him to call out in surprise. As it transpired this was not an isolated incident and he experienced it again the following night, this time on the back of his hand, which displayed all the signs of having been burned.

This event was followed by parallel scratch marks spontaneously appearing on his neck and hands as if a cat had clawed him. To compound matters he had moved to England six months prior to our visit where he stayed with his father and the 'attacks' continued, the most recent reported only a few days previously. Jane explained that her son had become romantically involved with a married woman with three children whose husband was currently imprisoned for armed robbery. The woman's husband had found out about the affair and although still imprisoned was threatening to have friends on the outside attack her son. It also emerged that her daughter, who is seventeen, was pregnant by an older man who did not treat her at all well.

With this in mind, I decided that there appeared to be a real need for assistance and to this end I contacted Andrew Wilson and his wife Pauline (pseudonyms), two talented mediums who assist on cases like this, and explained the situation. They felt that since the alleged 'attacks' were continuing when the son was not in the house, then it was certain that the problem resided in the son and not the building. The nature of the problem, whether it was an entity or the son's own uncontrolled psychic abilities, would not be resolved until they had the chance to talk with Jane. We agreed to meet at the house the following week in an attempt to neutralise the situation, although what occurred was much more than that

After we all arrived Jane briefly outlined the series of events to the psychics, after which they asked if they could check the house, and Jane gave them the go ahead. We started in her bedroom where the two mediums quickly detected areas of psychic energy, one of which was directly above her bed. I was invited to experience the affected area; I extended my hands into an 'energy field'. The temperature drop was sharp and unmistakable; there was even a subtle variation in the 'texture' of the air.

This sounds rather odd and is totally subjective, but nevertheless there seemed to be a slight resistance in the areas of cold. I was using a video camera as a kind of real time diary recording the events as they occurred, but when I pointed it at the area of 'psychic energy' the auto focus would not work and the lens cycled back and forward looking for a point to settle on. I pointed it elsewhere and it focussed right away, but when I turned to the energy field again it refused to focus. This is not the first time that electronic equipment has misbehaved in situations like this, and it may well be a factor of how the phenomenon functions.

Pauline looked rather uneasy and asked her husband if he could feel anything. He had already detected areas of energy in the room as well, but these were all high up, almost at ceiling level. As we moved through all the other upstairs rooms, the mediums sensed a degree of psychic energy in each one; again they were located high up near the ceiling. By this time Pauline was looking distinctly worried. I asked her what was wrong. She told me that in this instance there was a 'Lower Astral Entity' in the house and it was imperative that they carry out an immediate cleansing ritual to remove it.

This entity had been 'feeding' off the negativity from this family for several years and was almost certainly the cause of the emotional strife within it. Moving downstairs we checked the other rooms. Pauline noticed a fleeting black shape as she opened the bathroom door. Unfortunately, although I was with them every step of the way recording the proceedings, I did not witness this, although to be fair I was not best placed to see it. When we had finished the checks, the medium explained her interpretation of the cause of the problems to Jane, and how she recommended dealing with it. Jane, although taken aback, readily agreed to the cleansing ceremony, so the medium asked for some salt and water, which was quickly provided.

I had never previously witnessed anything like this before so it was of particular interest to me. As mentioned at the beginning of the chapter, the salt and water are part of the traditional tools associated with exorcism and the belief comes from the use of water as a purifying and cleansing agent and salt being a substance used to preserve meat. Taken from another more practical perspective, a solution of salt and water makes an excellent conductor of electricity and once again, as with the malfunctioning electronic equipment, this may or may not be relevant to what these entities are and how they function.

The Cleansing

We all moved back upstairs again where, after securing all the windows, Pauline and her husband proceeded to sprinkle the salt and water solution at the entrance to each room, and then closed the doors. This, they explained, would seal each area and prevent the entity from escaping only to return when we had gone. We descended the stairs, repeating the cleansing procedure at the entrances to all the downstairs rooms, eventually gathering together in the living room once this final door had also been sealed. To ensure no interruptions, the mediums asked for the 'phone to be taken off the hook and the TV switched off. The psychics explained that their guides, their 'spirit helpers', would remove the offending spirit and return it to the astral plane. This is as good an explanation as any because whatever they do

---

Note It is worth explaining that according to the psychics Lower Astral Entities originate from the astral plane. The function of the astral plane apparently serves much the same purpose as the belief in Heaven, Purgatory and Hell espoused in Roman Catholic dogma, except that rather than three states of afterlife, the astral plane contains a far greater number. As a rule of thumb the worse you are in life, in death the further down the astral you descend. In common with conventional Catholic belief only by means of time and genuine repentance can one rise through the levels until eventually the spirit attains a variety of heaven. Whether this is the case or not hardly matters, all that really matters is that wherever they come from they can be forced to return.

it evidently works, but it would be fascinating to have a clearer understanding of the mechanics behind it. The mediums are quite happy to use their own terms of reference when discussing the subject, although this does tend to obscure in a cloak of mysticism, which can create a degree of confusion.

We sat in silence, and after a few moments meditation Pauline leaned back in her chair and her head dropped forward on to her chest, her breathing became slow and even. A few moments later the house began to reverberate with a dull thudding sound, then a loud scratching sound began to emanate from the walls and then the sound of movement could be heard from the bedroom directly overhead. We then heard slow footsteps descending the staircase and approaching the room we were in; then they stopped. I asked if it was possible (or even prudent) to open the door, but the other medium who was not in trance said an emphatic 'No', because although the ritual was working, any attempt to recognise the reality of the entity could empower it and even cause it to attach itself to whoever it deemed the most suitable. The atmosphere in the room became tense and charged, and the presence of the entity on the other side of the door caused feelings of intense anxiety.

We all looked at the medium who sat with her eyes closed apparently quite calm. Even in the low light levels in the room it was obvious that she had become deathly pale, and her eyelids looked almost black. Her husband watched her intently and with concern, although I had worked with them several times previously I had never seen him quite so worried. The medium began to breathe really deeply and her eyes opened, but she did not seem to register anything in the room, her attention was elsewhere. A few moments later several things occurred simultaneously, the medium sighed heavily, there was sharp, single knock on the door accompanied by what sounded like a sharp, almost anguished cry, a cup that was sitting on a coffee table slid along the surface and fell on the carpet, and the ceiling light began swinging to and fro. At that point the medium sat back in her chair again, and - visibly relaxed - she told us that the entity had gone, and indeed there was a palpable sense of change and relief in the room; everyone seemed more at ease. She then lifted a photograph of Jane's son and held it between her hands. Her eyes closed and her head drooped forward in concentration as she sent her guides to help the boy, as it later transpired she evidently achieved a result. Before we returned to re-check the other rooms to make certain that all the energy had dissipated, the psychics chatted to Jane. What was revealed proved a profoundly moving experience for all of us. It was obvious from the conversation that Jane had not had an easy life, and really only wanted some peace.

Her husband had abandoned her early in the marriage and left her with two young children to raise as best she could, so her life had been a continuous struggle. Pauline started to cry as she sensed some of the negative emotions surrounding Jane. She made it clear to us that many unpleasant things had occurred in Jane's life, but due to their nature could not be discussed in the present situation; it is enough to say that Jane's life had been neither pleasant nor happy. The medium also explained that the misfortunes in the lives of Jane's children were also directly attributable to the negative emanations from the entity. The spirit had evidently latched on to the family during the early years of her marriage. Without going into too much detail, almost from birth the son had witnessed his mother being subjected to a great deal of mental, physical and verbal abuse. This had affected him on various levels, driving his spirit down until he became open to the malevolent attentions of a negative entity. This evil creature had been with the family for around seventeen years working its malignant charms and dragging them all down in order to feed off their negative emotions. Now that it had been banished to whatever pit it had originally emerged from, the entire family would benefit. As the negative influences faded away, her son who was still staying in England with his father, yet another source of negativity, would eventually want to move back to be near her. As an added bonus, Pauline told Jane that she would leave an 'angel' with her to help her on a spiritual level. The angel, she explained, was a male named 'Faith', and if Jane asked for help he would guide and protect her.

For the record, there are some aspects of this work that are not testable in any meaningful way. For example, I cannot say that there was an angel there, nor can I say there was not. In a case like this, other than the taped evidence and the emotional sensations, there is not one iota of objective proof to offer. If it helped Jane then that's fine and if it didn't, well, no harm was done. The only point I can make is this, when we entered Jane's bedroom after the cleansing, all sensations of 'cold spots' and temperature fluctuations over her bed had gone. The entire house felt 'different', much calmer and warmer and the improvement in Jane was patently obvious. Regarding the 'angel', I have no views on this aspect of the investigation, different people refer to various things using different names, and this is one such example. As the reader will have noticed in their own experience, there are many examples where placebos may be as effective as real events.

Was this an exorcism by any other name? The answer to that has to be yes! Was it entirely psychological or had some aspect of reality been altered? Can mediums really contact negative entities and, in effect - like magicians of old - control them? What was the cause of the temperature drop above Jane's bed? Why did the air seem to have a texture? Why was there a pool of water under Jane's bed and why was her mattress soaking wet? Why did all these conditions alter after the cleansing? Unfortunately, all I can offer are supposition, conjecture and an account of what I saw, but not definitive answers. Whether real or imagined, changes had taken place during a three-hour period, and changes for the better. We later discovered that, as Pauline had predicted, both of Jane's children returned to their mother and were staying with her. Interestingly, the 'attacks' on her son ceased immediately prior to his return home and after the cleansing took place, and - more importantly - the house was still peaceful.

PART THREE

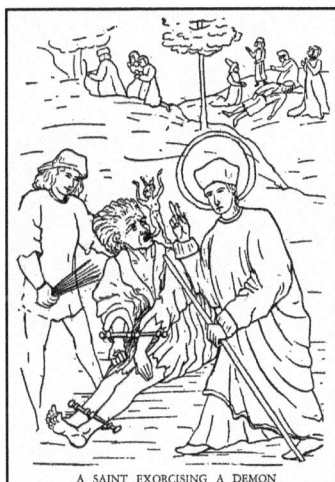

A SAINT EXORCISING A DEMON

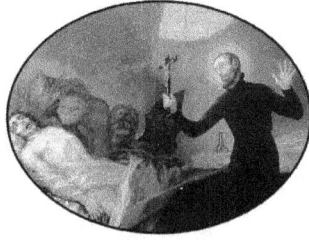

Chapter 36
Possession; The Alternatives

In fairness to this fascinating subject we have to consider options other than apparently genuine possession. One area that is inextricably linked to possession, and of course the methods by which the possessing entity is removed, is psychiatry because there are a range of medical conditions that can produce symptoms identical to those of genuine possession. First and foremost we have to accept the basic premise that psychiatry does not, and indeed cannot, acknowledge the existence of demonic possession of a human being as a legitimate medical condition.

While true that the psychiatric profession cannot recognise the condition formally, there are some psychiatrists who are also involved with aspects of fundamentalist Christianity who will accept that possession can and does occur. As for the others, in their opinion they quite rightly cannot do so because it would open their profession to accusations of quackery and belief in the reality of supernatural phenomena, and that this can somehow interact with human beings in the real world. Any formal diagnosis made has to be of a legitimate psychiatric condition, which may, or may not, respond to treatment using drugs and/or therapy.

The condition that is most frequently presented as an alternative to demonic possession is that of 'Multiple Personality Disorder', which is now known as 'Disassociated Identify Disorder' or 'DID' and we will use this term to describe manifestations of this condition. DID can manifest in a number of ways, but mainly through the appearance of several distinctly different personalities manifesting in an individual. The number of these personalities (called 'alters' and derived from the term 'alternative personalities') can vary wildly from patient to patient, and can range from one alter to anything up to a thousand.

The really bizarre thing about this condition is that each alter speaks with a different voice, has different likes and dislikes, can be of a different sex, has different handwriting and different names. Some therapists claim that they have uncovered different animal species (possible I suppose if one takes the view that human beings are also animals, albeit highly evolved) as well and, almost unbelievably, even vegetable personalities.

However, some of the alters occasionally describe themselves as demons, which serves to muddy the waters still further, and it is easy to see why clergymen might be tempted to conduct exorcisms, especially if they encountered the person/alter with no prior knowledge of the condition. It would be even worse in the days before psychiatry developed and recognised that these conditions existed at all, in which case, as we have seen elsewhere, the person so afflicted would automatically be assumed possessed by an evil spirit.

One slightly worrying thing about this is that, just perhaps, the possessing entity is being rationalised away as a medical condition when it is not. The other thing is that perhaps the 'alter' in question is well aware of what it is doing and is deliberately choosing to call itself a demon in the interests of mischief making. It also serves to illustrate just how complex the human brain really is, we can map it and measure it, but it still continues to confound the 'experts' who, if they are honest, still do not understand how consciousness really functions, let alone what it is.

There are, however, some problems linked to DID and in some cases sufferers are not ill at all, but demand attention and do so by displaying these symptoms, although that said, to demand that level of attention is surely a medically significant condition in itself. It has also been suggested that DID is created by the psychiatric therapy undergone by some people. This may be the result of some therapists indulging in the highly controversial technique of 'recovered memories', which has resulted in claims of Satanic ritual abuse among other things. It may be that the patient is trying to rationalise what the therapist is saying and can only do so by creating another personality to fulfil the suggestions.

One anti-cult Christian fundamentalist group has said that some individuals appear to have a mixture of alters and possessing demons, and it is absolutely vital to separate the two in order to provide healing for both conditions. This may well be correct, but if both conditions responded favourably to suitable medication this must surely call into question the demonic aspect for the symptoms. As with much of what has been said in this book, one cannot simply dismiss the possibility of possession by evil spirits, since consciousness, the human brain and what it is capable of is still an unknown. Perhaps the medications reduce the susceptibility of the individual to possession; perhaps they act like an analogue of the salt and water used in exorcism.

In a similar vein, those who subscribe to the Christian practise of deliverance ministry as a form of exorcism are sure that the 'born again' members of their faith cannot be demonically possessed. They hold this view because by their logic (if logic can be applied to this illogical phenomenon) once the person has been born again and saved, the 'Holy Spirit' has filled them and demons cannot then enter. This leads to the automatic and highly polarised assumption that since they are surrounded by billions of individuals who have not been born again and saved, (which therefore must include all non-Christians as well) they are open to demonic attack. This exactly parallels the very similar view that since Christ is supposed to have said that, 'the only way to the father is through me', all non-Christians are doomed anyway, whether possessed or not.

On the other hand there can be occasions where the cause and the effect of possession and related phenomena can be quite unexpected and come from a completely unexpected quarter lying somewhere in between the cracks of reality and spirituality. Although the subject matter of this chapter may ostensibly have relevance to the enigma of unidentified flying objects (UFOs), it may also be remarkably relevant to the process of possession, and how it relates to external forces that can affect the processes of the human brain and produce various personalities. This is so because it has been claimed that some individuals, admittedly a very few, claim to have been possessed by non-human 'alters' that originated in the far reaches of the universe.

There have been many reasons posited for the bizarre and unwelcome phenomenon of alien (demonic) abduction; everything from actual kidnapping by extraterrestrials (demons) to plain attention seeking by the person(s) involved. However, one of the most thought provoking and readily provable explanations is the hypothesis that the abduction scenario is the product of two factors: electrochemical imbalances and common neural hardwiring in the human brain. This concept sits snugly within the discipline and framework of psychiatry and has been pioneered for many years by several researchers who experienced a largely uphill struggle against die-hard believers in the ETH (Extraterrestrial Hypothesis), and others, who for a variety of reasons flatly refuse to accept that this is a viable, alternative explanation.

The electromagnetic approach to alien abduction developed out of earlier research into the related phenomena of ghost and poltergeist manifestations carried out by Albert Budden and others

The work of researchers like Dr. Michael Persinger, Professor of Neuroscience at the Laurentian University in Canada, and Professor Kenneth Ring (among others), have positively identified that exposure to relatively weak electromagnetic (EM) fields has a pronounced effect on human neurophysiology. Based on this research, it is clear that a range of hallucinations can be induced artificially by introducing EM fields (in most cases using small permanent magnets external to the skull) into the close vicinity of specific areas in the brain (i.e. the temporal lobes, the hippocampus and the amygdala, all of which are components of the limbic system).

The temporal lobes (one of the most electrically unstable areas of the brain) are particularly relevant here, because it is this area that appears to be central in a number of paranormal encounters. There are many reports where people have woken from sleep, unable to move and convinced that there is a frightening, invisible presence in the room with them. This is almost certainly due to electrical malfunctions in the temporal lobes induced by the presence of EM fields from a variety of sources.

During a recent neurosurgical procedure conducted during 2002 in Sweden, the surgeons discovered that when specific areas of the brain surface were touched with electrodes carrying a very weak electrical charge, the recipient experienced a range of odd sensory impressions. The fact that the patient was not fully anaesthetised is not uncommon in some neurological procedures, because the brain itself has no pain receptors. These included out of body experiences (OBEs), where the patient (in this instance a woman), felt herself floating near the ceiling of the operating theatre looking down at both her body and the surgical team. As well as having the strong impression that an invisible presence was watching her, she also experienced the almost obligatory sensation of being drawn towards a tunnel of light. While falling within the parameters of other, similar reported incidents, as we shall see there may be more than the influence of electrical neural stimulation at work here.

It is particularly important to realise that it is not only artificial EM fields that can cause sightings of ghosts, aliens and demons. Prior to the creation of this type of radiation the main source of EM energy derived from naturally occurring geological elements like magnetic ores and other factors including random lightening strikes etc., it is often the case that when accounts of long standing 'haunted' sites are examined there is evidence of geological faulting below the area. These faults give rise to slight tectonic movements, which in turn generate EM energy.

Factors like this played a vital role in certain sightings predating the arrival of man-made radiation and tended to affect the perceptions of people who were sensitive to electrical fields. On the other hand, accounts of modern hauntings etc., often reveal the presence of artificial EM 'hotspots'. These are created by the proximity of a variety of sources including high-tension power lines, radar - both civilian and military - Cellphones and Cellphone masts, radio antennae, domestic appliances, faulty household wiring, geomagnetism and even microwave emissions from satellites etc., and sometimes a combination of them all. This is something that, to my knowledge, has never been factored into examinations of the circumstances surrounding cases of possession.

Although not directly pertaining to possession, nevertheless it is still in the same general ballpark and in terms of the abduction scenario other factors have become apparent in cases of CEIV, or close encounters of the fourth kind. This term refers to people who not only have seen extraterrestrials, but also have physically been abducted by them, either by persuasion, coercion or physical force. The late UFO researcher Dr Allen Hynek devised the CE (close encounter) scale to cover a spectrum of ET experiences ranging from CEI, (close encounter of the first kind) which encompasses basic sightings of UFOs through CEII and III to CEIV.

Each classification describes an increasing level of involvement with both ETs and their craft. Might the classifications of contact also describe degrees of possession? Another factor not generally appreciated with the ET/Demon interface is the simple fact that many of these creatures are, for all intents and purposes, identical in appearance. This introduces the 'Arthur C. Clark factor', where any sufficiently advanced technology is indistinguishable from magick, and the abilities of some ETs are synonymous with those of demons, but in the case of ET this is due to technology.

The EM explanation suggests that small particles of cellular magnetite called 'magnetosomes' become lodged in the human body, especially in the sinus cavity where it gathers in larger quantities. This substance becomes magnetised during exposure to accidental electrical traumas creating a small, permanent magnet, which - when in the sinus cavity - is situated immediately below the already electrically unstable temporal lobes. The reason for the nosebleeds is also attributable to the small clumps of magnetite. When exposed to external EM fields, the magnetite rotates, thereby creating a phenomenon called a 'gyromagnetic disturbance'. This is similar to the rotation of the shaft in an electric motor and the result is tissue can be torn releasing blood, which in turn flows from the nose. Note that blood is also seen to flow spontaneously from the possessed and of course those who are alleged to display signs of stigmata, i.e. bearing visible marks of the passion of Christ.

Regarding hallucinations produced by magnetic fields, as recently as 1992 when traces of magnetite were detected in brain cells, it was discovered that when in the presence of a magnetic field the magnetite aligns itself with the magnetic field and begins to vibrate. The vibration (or resonance) causes the surface of the brain cells to ionise releasing specific ions; these in turn cause the release of a variety of neurotransmitters, e.g. serotonin and dimethyltryptamine. It is these neurotransmitters that create a variety of hallucinations based on common neural 'hardwiring' within the brain; these include the classic symptoms of demonic possession. It is worth noting that dimethyltryptamine is the active component of the traditional shamanic hallucinogen Ayhuasca.

Aside from allergic reactions to EM fields and their affects on certain areas of the brain, there is another more worrying factor involved. In the mid 1990s Professor Ring, whilst attached to the psychology dept of Connecticut University, conducted a series of in-depth examinations into the lives of CEIV experiencers. Prof. Ring's investigations built upon earlier evidence suggesting that many people who claim to have experienced CEIV encounters; in addition to being unusually sensitive to EM fields, have also been victims of systematic childhood abuse. His findings were published in the book, *The Omega Project* by Kenneth Ring [pub William Morrow, USA, 1992]. This evidence is particularly interesting for several reasons; the child, as a reaction to continual stress creates a discrete, self-contained, inner fantasy life.

The result of this self-conditioning creates a subjective, virtual reality, defence mechanism that can be accessed as an automatic process that is analogous to changing the channel on a TV set when the programme is unsuitable. The difference in this case is the viewer/experiencer is totally immersed in it and is part of the new programme. It has to be stressed that the people affected by repeated alien abduction encounters and paranormal episodes have already been sensitised to EM radiation, and in many cases go on to become 'serial abductees'. This condition does not affect the vast majority of persons who are not sensitised. Incidentally, this process of abuse is deliberately exploited as a component in a 'brain washing' technique called 'compartmentalisation', which is used by intelligence (and other) covert agencies to induce mind control through trauma. It is this that may most closely resemble what is occurring to people who exhibit signs of possession.

The subject is brutally and repeatedly traumatised until the mind, in an act of sheer self-preservation, creates a safe haven to protect itself from further abuse. Once in this condition, by means of a signal often comprising key words or phrases, the abuser/controller then effectively programmes the subject to carry out whatever actions are required of them. The process is particularly effective on the very young and it is perhaps from this that charges of Satanic Ritual Abuse emerged. The subject while in the altered state will carry out their instructions with no memory of having done so. Another factor recently discovered in the neurobiological makeup of abductees, are physical differences in the brain structure brought about by the childhood abuse. The continued stress during the formative years releases a neurotransmitter called 'cortisol', which sculpts the brain, producing observable physical differences in an especially electrically irritable limbic system capable of producing a wide range of hallucinations when under stress.

Corroboration for these findings comes from research conducted by an American neurobiologist Dr. Martin Teicher, who measured brain-wave activity in 115 consecutive admissions to a child and psychiatric hospital. *'We found significant brain-wave abnormalities in 54% of patients with a history of early trauma, but only 27% of non-abused patients'*. [*The Scars That Won't Heal: The Neurobiology of Child Abuse* Martin H. Teicher, Scientific American. March 2002, pp. 54-61]. Also significant is the following comment from the same article *'We observed EEH abnormalities in 72% of those who had documented histories of serious physical and sexual abuse. The irregularities arose in frontal and temporal brain regions and to our surprise, specifically involved the left hemisphere rather than both sides as one would expect'* [Ibid.]

Fortunately, Teicher was also able to corroborate his own work: *'Subsequent work by other investigators using magnetic resonance imaging (MRI) technology has confirmed an association between early maltreatment and reductions in the size of the adult hippocampus. The amygdala may be smaller as well'* [Ibid.] Also quoting previous investigations he states: *'Our findings dovetailed with a 1978 EEG (electro-encephalogram) study of adults who were victims of incest. The study's author, Robert W. Davies of the Yale University School of Medicine and his team found that 77% exhibited EEG abnormalities and 27% experienced seizures'* [Ibid.]. Although electroencephalographs (EEG) have been performed on those exhibiting signs of possession, they did not show any pathological findings including epileptic discharges, but indicated enhanced power in the theta and alpha ranges in the brain during the trance.

It is clear that in addition to temporal lobe epilepsy, a significant factor in CEIV (and now apparently possession) experience may be directly attributable to malfunctions within specific areas of the brains of those experiencing both CEIV and paranormal/demonic encounters. Having said that, it is also possible that people who are electrically hypersensitive (EH) could have elevated psychic abilities as well. This, once again, might be an explanation of why some of those who are 'possessed' can display a range of apparently 'supernatural' abilities. However, it is also fair to say that any ability that seems to fly in the face of accepted physics might well deserve to be called 'supernatural' until a demonstrably reasonable and rational explanation can be found, and in most cases that has not yet occurred.

It is difficult to say precisely why this should be the case, but it is possible that some latent ability within the human brain is triggered, i.e. 'switched on' by EM irradiation and remains in this state. Whilst extremely difficult - if not impossible - to prove, there are many accounts indicating that mediums and psychics are in fact EH. In cases where EH is not obviously present, perhaps the person involved was born with the latent ability already fully functional and therefore did not require to be 'jump started'.

Likewise, while it is now known that the presence of EM fields triggers the release of neurotransmitters, it is also possible that these neurotransmitters, rather than producing a purely objective alteration in brain function, actually project the person affected into an altered state of awareness. While many will argue that all PSI talents, and that includes possession and exorcism, are non-existent, it appears logical that since the human brain is an organic electrochemical device, then, if - as has been suggested - we are surrounded by oceans of information, (the *'Morphogenetic fields'* proposed by Prof. Rupert Sheldrake), then perhaps in certain circumstances we can sample and process this information in various forms.

Serious researchers freely admit that there are numerous instances where conventional science fails to explain some PSI manifestations like clairvoyance, mediumship, apparitions and some classes of poltergeist phenomena and demonic possession etc. Therefore, interaction at a non-physical level between the mind and the electromagnetic universe cannot be ruled out, and is more likely than not perhaps a mixture of quantum science and metaphysics can supply some of the answers.

Chapter 37
Luon, Loudon and Exorcism : What to make of it.

Regarding the events that occurred at Luon and Loudon, we should keep in mind that the two examples of supposed demonic possession and exorcism that occurred there had additional back-stories that are not generally acknowledged. As we saw at Luon there was repeated mention of the Huguenots (especially from Beelzebub who announced that he was their prince) during the exorcism. The Catholic Church was fighting a battle to retain its grip (and therefore power and influence) over the population and anything that threatened this had to be resisted at all costs. Why else should the supposed demon announce that it was a Huguenot, and why should the demons that had been expelled set off for Geneva? Geneva was of course a centre of the Protestant faith!

In fact, during the exchanges between the Bishop and 'Beelzebub' the demon stated that the Huguenots were evil and desecrated communion wafers, this may seen inconsequential to us, but at that time it was a grave crime. The entity continued on this line by stating that the Huguenots would do more harm to Christ than the Jews had done. Obviously the Church could settle several scores here by showing conclusively that it had God on its side by driving out Satanic entities and at the same time demonstrate that the Huguenots were in league with the devil. The turbulent and fearful times in which all this happened has to be kept firmly in mind when judging whether or not there ever was any demonic possession at all, or the whole thing was stage managed and orchestrated by the Church.

The Loudon affair also had aspects that might raise some suspicions, the antipathy and open hostility felt towards Urbain Grandier by his superiors being the main one. In addition to that was the possibility that the accusations levelled at the unfortunate priest might well have been occasioned by the ravings of a woman fixated on him, but whose repressed sexual urges were unfulfilled. It is known that hysteria can and does have many unexpected and dramatic side effects on those affected, especially religious hysteria. Events related to forms of hysteria have been recorded in other convents and womens' (and men's) prisons so the effect is real.

Another instance of what may well be a form of possession often takes place in the polar regions among the Inuit and is called 'Arctic Hysteria', where the sufferers, normally females, exhibit all the classic signs of possession, but this almost always occurs during the especially harsh winter months. The condition, which the Inuit call *'pibloktoq,'* manifests as stripping naked, shrieking, howling and running wild in the sub-zero frozen wastes. This seems to derive from the related term, *'pivdlerortok'*, the Inuit word for an insane or delirious person, but nevertheless the Inuit also have their own strain of shamanism, which they use to (normally successfully) treat the conditions. It is possible that this is a more pronounced form of the 'cabin fever' often experienced when individuals or groups are cooped up in a confined space with nothing to do and are unable to get out in the outside world.

However, there are still aspects of both cases that leave a measure of doubt, but in the case of 'Robbie', the boy used as *The Exorcist* film template, there was no obvious axe to grind or reason for point scoring by any of those involved. This appears to be what it claimed to be; a genuine case of possession by 'something' that was eventually forced to leave the body of the youngster involved. Again there are many questions to be asked, particularly what actually does the possessing? How does 'it' get in and why is one particular person selected? Is it through physical weakness, lack of faith or is it none of these? Is the entire body possessed or just the brain?

This last option would appear to be the best guess here, because since the mind controls the body then once that has been successfully overpowered the rest would be relatively easy. Of course, this would not, and cannot, explain many of the manifestations like the alleged levitations and the spontaneous movement of items of furniture and ornaments etc. Then there are the loud and spontaneous noises so typical of poltergeist manifestations and the anomalous voices, what might cause these?

Phenomena like levitation has also been attributed to many saints, i.e. St Theresa of Avilla and St Thomas of Cupertino. Surely nothing demonic here, so what is occurring? Certainly a demonstration of some unknown, but powerful, force at work, but originating where; in the body of the person afflicted or an external source? It is a pity that it no longer seems to occur, or at least it is not reported because we could learn so much. Questions, always more questions, and sadly there is no conclusive answer to many of these events and each should be viewed on its own merits, but the one thing that shines through is this. As long as we have the desire to explore the secrets of the human condition and learn then that the impossible eventually becomes possible and the unknown known; we only need patience and curiosity.

The claims of deliverance and/or exorcism made by the various proponents of the evangelical religious right wing in the United States of America and elsewhere, what about that? Are they genuine exorcisms or are they the hysterical outpourings of people who are emotionally aroused and in an already suggestible state prodded on by charismatic preachers who don't know when to stop. Heaven forbid that they are actually and consciously exploiting these poor people for their own selfish ends, but given how they operate, that possibility is tantalisingly there too. Do they think they are actually 'saving' them from the predations of Satan, or are they simply lining their pockets at the expense of the gullible?

As we have already seen, a little research will amply demonstrate that none of these people are exactly poor and many are multi-millionaires enjoying an exceedingly lavish lifestyle in the manner of the super rich. Hardly a Spartan life for them, unlike that of the man they claim to promote. Unfortunately one has to conclude that anything 'miraculous' emanating for these ministries is unlikely to be genuine and only the physical result of impassioned motivational speaking that can indeed produce some remarkable short term results.

However, in spite of all the show and sham and the inevitable hucksters there is one last possibility, perhaps some of what occurred was genuine and perhaps some people really were possessed by some invisible entity. One of the main precepts of magick, especially chaos magick, which is perhaps the foundation of all magickal processes since the beginning of time, is the axiom of 'fake it till you make it'. In other words if you are convinced utterly that something can be made to happen then it is conceivable that reality can be edited to suit the will of the person making the wish.

At the risk of being repetitive, one of the best known of the modern magicians was the notorious Aleister Crowley (I cannot overstate just how pivotal to the subject this man is) and for all the ceremonial accoutrements that went with his flamboyant style of sorcery he knew that sufficient application of the human will could, and would, alter subjective reality. His famous dictum (paraphrased from Rabelais) *'Do what thou wilt shall be the whole of the Law. Love is the law, love under will'* says it all, even if it became slightly altered in the process.

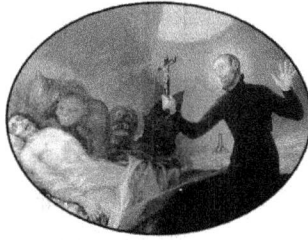

Chapter 38
Reality and Magick

There are three or perhaps four kinds of reality; objective (internal), subjective (external), consensus (collective) and mathematical and of these the only one that might snap the bonds that weld the fabric of reality together is the mathematical model of reality. The reason is surprisingly easy to grasp, although the mechanism by which this might happen much less so. The reason is in the ability of mathematics (or particle physics, in this case the two are inextricably linked) to describe down to the last subatomic particle what reality is and how we interact with the invisible forces that surround us.

The other three are based on opinions and the limitations of language which, although a formidable tool for communication, has inherent limitations. How, for example, can the physical impressions and intense feelings that emotions produce ever be adequately explained by language? Even the words on this page are open to interpretation and degree, so how can any author, no matter how well intentioned, ever be sure their words will have the effect, or convey the message they intend? It is likely, therefore, that the reality of magick is subjective and if the individual believes that it is real then it is, and if they believe strongly enough then it becomes real to everyone else. We should not forget that possession and exorcism are both related forms of magick so the same rules apply.

The best example of this is the entity known as the 'tulpa', which is a thought form brought into existence by a lengthy process of meditative and visualisation techniques. The classic case is the one described by the French born traveller Mme. Alexandra David-Neel while journeying in Tibet when a tulpa was created that looked exactly like one of the locals. It should be made clear that Mme David-Neel was an accomplished magician and practitioner of Tantrism in her own right and had a first class knowledge of the more esoteric aspects of Buddhism. The tulpa, initially at least, was affable enough, but eventually became hostile and unruly, and she spent almost six months dissipating it/him, There is no other way of saying it, she caused it to vanish as mysteriously as she had caused it to materialise, and all done though the power of the will.

In the course of this book we have encountered various ways in which possession is thought to take place, and not surprisingly one of the causes has been directly attributed to the lifestyle we currently lead, especially the young. According to Fr. Jeremy Davies, the Roman Catholic exorcist for the diocese of Westminster in London, England, increasing levels of promiscuity, homosexuality, contraception, abortion played their unsavoury and unwholesome part. As well as the physical side of the problem, he also included increased interest in spirituality, mediumship, yoga and other techniques imported from other belief systems, in other words the New Age fashion for spirituality. The use of Ouija boards (which, incidentally, are not something to be trifled with because the end results can be truly alarming) is also singled out, because according to Fr. Davies, *"They are direct invitations to the devil which he readily accepts"*.

While Rev Davies might be a little polarised in his views I have a degree of sympathy here, because using one of these devices (which, incredibly, were once sold as toys) has been likened to holding a party with everyone and anyone invited, a kind of psychic 'open house'. I have attended séances where they were used and have seen individuals terrified by the information they received, although very little of it seemed to be true. It has also been said that the entities who are contacted by this method seem to have a remarkably warped sense of humour and appear to be blatant liars as well who enjoy upsetting people. Perhaps this is another riff on the 'psychic vampires' hypothesis and they relish wallowing in the negative energies they create.

The Rev Davies also cites meditative techniques that have their roots in eastern mysticism as being the thin edge of the wedge allowing Satan to slip in unnoticed; for some reason he includes the use of beneficial techniques like acupuncture in this general heading. One point raised by Rev Davies does contain more than a kernel of truth however; he observes that, *"Sanity depends on our relationship to reality"*, and he is of course absolutely correct, because reality can be different depending on one's state of mind at any one time, although not any less 'real'. For example the reality of shamanic trances, irrespective of how they are produced, bear no relation to physical reality, but are no less valid for all that, especially if the shaman can produce some truly astonishing insights and information gleaned in their altered states. Wherever the shaman has gone under trance does not have to be in any way connected to anything Satanic or demonic and might even be an encounter with an aspect of the biblical God. In a final swipe at the Godless he also mentions Islam, Mormonism and the Korean Moonies cult as being good examples of the *'false and heretical prophets'* that are gradually but steadily leading Europe into a state of apostasy.

One more fascinating, if unlikely, method by which possession can occur in modern times involves computers, especially those built after 1985, because only they have sufficient memory and processing power to give sanctuary to an invading demon or evil spirit. This startling announcement came from the Rev Jim Peasboro (an evangelical Christian) who learned of the potential problem after having to counsel some of his congregation. The Rev became convinced that the use of computers was a sure way to be contacted by dark forces and tempted away from the path of righteousness. The demons infesting (possessing?) some computers were inducing the formerly good husbands and fathers to trawl through pornographic websites and other material. Faithful wives and mothers were logging on to chat rooms and indulging in shameless and obscene exchanges with complete strangers with no thought of any negative outcome.

Rev Peasboro goes on to explain that he logged on to the computer of the person being afflicted and was startled when the machine openly mocked him and displayed the message, *"Preacher, you are a weakling and you're god is a damned liar"*. Evidently the PC then started printing out what looked like a collection of random groups of letters. The concerned pastor passed them to an expert in languages who told him that the letters were in fact a stream of obscenities written in a long dead Mesopotamian dialect. While at first sight these claims seem laughable, if we pause for moment to consider that the human brain is an organic electrochemical machine, and computers are also delicate electronic devices, then a grey area appears.

I have commented elsewhere that demonic entities may be a part of the electromagnetic spectrum and if so may hypothetically be able to interact with the neural networks that allow our brains to function. If so, might it be possible that this is how they 'possess' a human being and exert control over them? If that is a valid hypothesis then might they also be able to impose themselves onto the microcircuits that form the computer's processors? If looked at in that manner, despite how 'out there' or unlikely it might seem, then perhaps the assertions made by the Rev Peasboro might not be regarded as totally insane. In a strange corollary to these claims are those made by the Rev David Hope, Archbishop of Westminster who warned that technology and computer wizardry was *"creating a society without a soul"*. He also states that the increased use of the Internet may be destroying our ability to function and interact socially. Given that we see so many signs of insularity and loneliness around us he may well have a point.

Chapter 39
Quantum Jumping

Perhaps the very last (and latest) word on updated magick and how cleansings, healings, vast riches and much else besides can be yours with little effort, comes from a strange belief system called 'quantum jumping' invented by Burt Goldman. This original take on one of the many highly esoteric facets of quantum physics promises just as much, if not more, than any of the so-called religions promoting Prosperity Theology by allowing the user to attract wealth and work miracles. Its only saving grace is that at least it does not try to use the fig leaf of faith to justify its claims, although, that said, depending on how one looks at it perhaps it does, so what's it all about? The 'quantum jumping' way to wealth and success relies on one facet among many of the theories relating to particle physics, and that is the proposition that there are an almost infinite number of versions of the universe out there, each of them containing another version of you.

The point that makes it all worthwhile is that at least one of these realities contains a much wealthier and prosperous you and all you need to do is tap into the reality and gather some of these benefits. Of course the downside is that there will be other versions of you that are destitute, but you can safely ignore them and concentrate on the positive aspects. Once you have made contact with the 'other you' via the subconscious mind all you have to do is ask the other you how they did it and if you have any sense you take that advice and get rich. This is of course assuming that the 'other you' is minded to share the secrets of their (your?) success. The technique also allows you to channel spiritual healing energy because at least one of your alternate versions will be able to do this too.

A well-known physicist once illustrated this point (not in connection with any scam I hasten to add) by this tale. One of his friends, a Russian physicist, was in Las Vegas and he had $100 at his disposal for use in the gambling casinos. As you can imagine in that context $100 is little more than what you would tip the croupier or waitress, it is by no means a lot of money. At any rate the Russian entered the first casino and placed the entire $100 bet on a single number on a roulette table: in a matter of seconds it was lost. The first physicist asked his friend why he had not spread the money around, only to be met with the reply that in another reality he won; in that situation the assertion is difficult to refute.

One *YouTube* clip shows Burt Goldman 'laying on hands', or in this case a scarf, and healing a man in his late '50s of rheumatic pain in his lower back. In fact, this is just another variant on the so-called 'green prayer cloth' scam touted by the televangelist Don Stewart as a miracle cure-all for what ails you. Other variations on this are the special faith soap and the olive oil from the Holy Land which apparently will bring about similar cures depending on how strong your faith happens to be...and as ever that is the driving factor here...faith...and perhaps money!

Appendices
Albert Buddens 25 Questions

There follows a list of the questions created by Albert Budden, designed to indicate the possible presence of electromagnetic hypersensitivity.

1. Do you frequently get severe shocks from door handles, car bodywork or other surfaces?
2. Do you feel uncomfortable in synthetic materials (e.g. acrylic, nylon)?
3. Are you sensitive to perfumed products, aerosols, cigarette smoke, petrol, gas, make-up, aftershave, etc.?
4. Does electrical equipment go wrong or behave oddly in your presence?
5. Are there any foods/drinks that you either avoid or consume large quantities of? Do you have food allergies (e.g. chocolate, coffee, milk, food with artificial coloring or flavors, wheat products)?
6. Did you have a happy childhood? If no, give reasons briefly.
7. Do you ever have hairs on your body stand on end, feel suddenly cold or overheated, experience tingling or numbness?
8. Do you ever get a metallic taste in your mouth?
9. Do you get *deja vu* strongly and often?
10. Do you ever get the overwhelming sensation that someone is in the room with you, watching, although you cannot see anyone?
11. Are you very sensitive to light? (Sunlight? Flickering light? Do you wear tinted glasses?)
12. Are you sensitive to any medications (especially antibiotics)?
13. Do you have what would be called psychic experiences (e.g. ghostly encounters, OBEs, etc.)?
14. Do you find that objects in your home go missing or behave oddly in any way?
15. Do light bulbs seem to last a very short period of time in your home?
16. Have you ever been close to a lightning strike or suffered major electrocution or defibrillation, or have you ever had electroconvulsive therapy/ECT?
17. Do you ever see small lights darting about the room?
18. Does fluorescent light bother you at all?

19. Do you ever have periods where you lose all concentration, feel overheated, see light flashes, lose muscle power in your legs and feel tingly and heavy?
20. Are there any of the following features near your home: a quarry, radio mast, power lines, reservoir, hill, military base, TV/radio station, radio ham?
21. Does time ever seem to slow down or pass in a flash?
22. Have you ever had periods of time for which you cannot account?
23. As an activity, do you write much?
24. Have you ever had the experience of everything going very still, timeless and silent?
25. Do you ever get painful electrical rippling sensations under the skin?

The English translation of the Latin *Rituale Romanum* First published in the reign of Paul V

This is the current version that was much disliked by Fr. Gabriel Amorth and his traditionalist brethren. The priest, robed in surplice and violet stole, one end of which is placed round the neck of the possessed person, bound if he is violent, sprinkles those present with holy water. Then the service begins. Note that the full ritual consists of three separate exorcisms each one slightly longer that the one before and all contain several firm demands that the invading spirit leave immediately. The † symbol indicates that the sign of the cross should be made.

- 1. *The Litany.*
- 2. *Psalm 54* ('Save me, O God, by Thy name').
- 3. *Adjuration* imploring God's grace for the proposed exorcism against the 'wicked dragon' and a caution to the possessing spirit to 'tell me thy name, the day, and the hour of thy going out by some sign.'
- 4. *The Gospel* (John I; and/or Mark XVI; Luke X; Luke XI).
- 5. *Preparatory Prayer.*

Then the priest, protecting himself and the possessed by the sign of the cross, placing part of his stole round the neck and placing his right hand on the head of the possessed, resolutely and with great faith shall say what follows.

6. *First Exorcism:*
'I exorcise thee, most vile spirit, the very embodiment of our enemy, the entire spectre, the whole legion, in the name of Jesus Christ, to † get out and flee from this creature of God ††.

'He Himself commands thee, who has ordered those cast down from the heights of heaven to the depths of the earth. He commands thee, he who commanded the sea, the winds, and the tempests.

'Hear therefore and fear, O Satan, enemy of the faith, foe to the human race, producer of death, thief of life, destroyer of justice, root of evils, kindler of vices, seducer of men, betrayer of nations, inciter of envy, origin of avarice, cause of discord, procurer of sorrows. Why dost thou stand and resist, when thou knowest that Christ the Lord will destroy they strength? Fear him who was immolated in Isaac, sold in Joseph, slain in the lamb, crucified in man, and then was triumphant over hell.

(The signs of the cross † should be made on the forehead of the possessed.)

'Depart therefore in the name of the † Father, and of the†† Son, and of the Holy † Ghost; give place to the Holy Ghost, by the sign of the † Cross of Jesus Christ our Lord, who with the Father and the same Holy Ghost liveth and reigneth one God, for ever and ever, world without end.'

- *7. Prayer for Success*, and making the signs of the cross over the demoniac.

8. Second Exorcism.
'I adjure thee, thou old serpent, by the judge of the quick and the dead, by thy maker and the maker of the world, by him who has power to send thee to hell, that thou depart quickly from this servant of God, N. (name of the possessed), who returns to the bosom of the Church, with fear and the affliction of thy terror. I adjure the again († on his forehead), not in my infirmity, but by the virtue of the Holy Ghost, that thou depart from this servant of God, N., whom Almighty God hath made in his own image.

'Yield therefore; yield not to me, but to the minister of Christ. For his power urges thee, who subjugated thee to his cross. Tremble at his arm, who led the souls to light after the lamentations of hell had been subdued. May the body of man be a terror to thee († on his chest), let the image of God be terrible to thee († on his forehead). Resist not, neither delay to flee from this man, since it has pleased Christ to dwell in this body. And, although thou knowest me to be none the less a sinner, do not think me contemptible.

- For it is God who commands thee †.
- The majesty of Christ commands thee †.
- God the Father commands thee †.
- God the Son commands thee †.
- God the Holy Ghost commands thee †.
- The sacred cross commands thee †.
- The faith of the holy apostles Peter and Paul and of all other saints commands thee †.
- The blood of the martyrs commands thee †.
- The constancy of the confessors commands thee †.

- The devout intercession of all saints commands thee †.
- The virtue of the mysteries of the Christian faith commands thee †.

'Go out, therefore, thou transgressor. Go out, thou seducer, full of all deceit and guile, enemy of virtue, persecutor of innocence. O most dire one, give place; give place, thou most impious; give place to Christ, in whom thou hast found nothing of thy works, who hath despoiled thee, who hath destroyed thy kingdom, who hath led thee captive and hath plundered thy goods, who hath cast thee into outer darkness, where for thee and they ministers is prepared annihilation.

But why, truculent one, dost thou withstand? Why, rash creature, dost thou refuse?
'
Thou art accused by Almighty God, whose statues thou hast transgressed.
'Thou art accused by his Son, Jesus Christ, our Lord, whom thou didst dare to tempt and presume to crucify.
'Thou art accused by the human race, to whom by the persuasion thou hast given to drink the poison of death.
'Therefore I adjure thee, most wicked dragon in the name of the † immaculate lamb, who trod upon the asp and basilisk, who trampled the lion and dragon, to depart from this man († let the sign be made on his forehead), to depart from the Church of God († let the sign be made on those standing by). Tremble and flee at the invocation of the name of that Lord at whom hell trembles, to whom the virtues of heaven, the powers and dominions are subject, whom cherubim and seraphim with unwearied voices praise, saying, Holy, holy, holy, Lord God of Sabbath.

- 'The word made flesh † commands thee'.
- 'He who was born of the Virgin † commands thee'.

Jesus of Nazareth commands thee, who, although thou dids despise his disciples, bade thee go, crushed and prostrate, out of the man, and in his presence, when he had separated thee from the man, thou didst not presume to go into a herd of swine.

'Therefore, adjured now in his † name, depart from this man, whom he has created. It is hard for thee to wish to resist. It is hard for thee to kick against the pricks †. Because the more slowly thou go out, the more the punishment against thee increases, since thou despisest not men but him who is Lord of the quick and dead, who shall come to judge the quick and the dead and the world by fire.'

- *9. Prayer for Success.*
- *10. Third and Final Exorcism:*

Therefore, I adjure thee, most vile of spirits, the entire spectre, the very embodiment of Satan, in the name of Jesus Christ † of Nazareth, who, after his baptism in Jordan, was led into the wilderness and overcame thee in thine own habitations, that thou stop assaulting him whom he hath formed from the dust of the earth to the honour of his glory, and that thou tremble not at the human weakness in miserable man but at the image of Almighty God.

Therefore, yield to God, who by his servant Moses drowned thee and thy malice in Pharaoh and in his army in the abyss.

Yield to God, who made thee flee when expelled from King Saul with spiritual songs through his most faithful servant, David.

Yield to God † who condemned thee in Judas Iscariot the traitor. For he beats thee with divine † scourges, in whose sight, trembling and crying out with thy legions, thou hast said: What are thou to us, O Jesus, Son of the most high God? Art thou come hither to torture us before our time? He presses on thee with perpetual flames, who shall say at the end of time to the wicked: Depart from me, ye cursed, into everlasting fire, which is prepared for the devil and his angels.

For thee, impious one, and for thy angels are prepared worms which never die.

For thee and thy angels is prepared the unquenchable fire; because thou art the chief of accursed murder, thou art the author of incest, the head of sacrilege, the master of the worst actions, the teacher of heretics, the inventor of all obscenities. Therefore, O impious one, go out. Go out, thou scoundrel, go out with all thy deceits, because God has willed that man be his temple.

But why dost thou delay longer here?

Give honour to God, the Father Almighty, to whom every knee is bent.

Give place to the Lord Jesus Christ † who shed for man his most precious blood.

Give place to the Holy Ghost, who through his blessed apostle Peter manifestly struck thee in Simon Magnus, who condemned thy deceit in Ananias and Sapphira, who smote thee in Herod the King because he did not give God honour, who through his apostle Paul destroyed thee in the magician Elymas by the mist of blindness, and through the same apostle by his word of command bade thee come out of the pythoness.

Now therefore depart. † Depart, thou seducer. Thy abode is the wilderness, thy habitation is the serpent. Be humbled and prostrate. Now there is no time to delay. For behold the Lord God approaches quickly, and his fire will glow before him and precede him and burn up his enemies on every side. For if thou hast deceived man, thou canst not mock God.

- 'He expels thee, from whose eye nothing is secret.
- 'He expels thee, to whose power all things are subject.
- 'He excludes thee, who has prepared for thee and thy angels everlasting hell; out of whose mouth the sharp sword will go, he who shall come to judge the quick and the dead and the world by fire.'

11. Final

The Rosslyn Frequencies

Mention was made of 'The Rosslyn Frequencies' in relation to the bizarre case that engulfed Terry Graham and her son while living in Guadalajara in Mexico. The mediums and I suggested she try using this particular frequency as an adjunct to removing whatever entity was manifesting itself in her home; so what are The Rosslyn Frequencies? These are a series of musical intervals, one of which is called an augmented fourth and they are present in the Chapel as engraved patterns in the stone cubes set in the ceiling of the Lady Chapel or 'retro-choir' located at the east end of the Chapel. I don't intend to go into the whys and wherefores of the Chapel because that has been done elsewhere in books devoted to the subject, but we do need to look at the patterned carved cubes in their own right.

The idea that these represent musical notes is not new and the first person to look at this possibility was the late hotelier and former MI5 operative Steven Prior, who was also apparently in charge of MI5's attempts at something along the lines of the CIA's Stargate Project. In the 1990s Mr Prior came to the conclusion that the patterns carved into the cubes represented musical notes and he commissioned a photographer, a musicologist and a computer programmer to try to decode the patterns into recognisable music. Unfortunately, Mr Prior, who was sure the notes represented a 'healing cadence', died before this came to fruition, but his work was enough to make interested parties aware of the possibility. In my own investigations into the Rosslyn enigma, I came to the conclusion that the carvings were in fact an early depiction of 'Chladni patterns' named after the German physicist Ernst Chladni.

Chladni devised a method of securing a thin metal plate, sprinkling fine sand on to the plate then 'playing' it with a bow such as would be used for a violin or similar. This had the effect of creating stress patterns that altered depending on the frequency of the note being played. It has been demonstrated that the stone cubes do indeed show carved frequency patterns and that the builder of the chapel, Sir William Sinclair, crucially would have had the means to recreate these patterns hundreds of years before Chladni, so, what does this mean? I have to own up here because my discovery was based on sheer luck, although in retrospect I now wonder if it was only luck or something else. I somehow guessed that the music was not all that important, but specific frequencies in it were, and this turned out to be correct. After some research I concluded that the hidden secret was an augmented fourth comprising the notes F#, C and A. Fortunately another researcher working independently, a musician, came to the same conclusion so there seemed to be a consensus.

Why use this note? Well the Catholic Church had proscribed its use throughout Europe in the Middle Ages on the grounds that the note caused feelings of unease and dissonance in some of those who heard it. Even worse by the standards of the Church, was that it might even have caused some who were especially susceptible to actually experience an altered state of consciousness. Given the surroundings where this occurred, i.e. a church, then the person so affected might even have 'seen God' or something else along these lines and this the Church could not, and would not, tolerate since it, and it alone, decided who would receive any spiritual revelations. To this end they called this particular chord the *'diablis et musica'* or the 'devil in music' and from there it became more widely known as 'The Devil's Chord'.

In my opinion, Sir William Sinclair decided to deliberately encode the note in the building as part of his plan to conceal something of immense importance in its structure. I also believe he constructed the most cunning hiding place ever devised, one that would be utterly undetectable unless both its location and the key to open it were revealed, and part of that 'key' in the Devil's Chord. My own experiences of using this musical interval inside Rosslyn Chapel indicated that the chapel may have been designed to use the frequency in a very unique manner and the building certainly reacted strangely to an experiment conducted in October 2005.

When the note was recreated the building produced two other harmonics entirely on its own, there was also an indication that there may well be a 'portal' in the chapel designed to open through the application of the note, plus a specific colour of light, but that is all described in detail in the book *Rosslyn, Between two Worlds*. That aside, the frequency has been used to very good effect by Patrick McNamara during séances, and it has also produced a range of effects in even casual listeners. This is why Patrick suggested we use it to help combat whatever was affecting Terry.

Mention is also made by Karl Fallon of the 'Gematria equivalent' tones in relation to the frequencies. Gematria is an ancient divinatory technique, which basically renders words into numbers; this remarkable science seems to show that words and phrases of similar meaning have an identical numerical value. This particular set of frequencies referred to by Karl was devised by Mr Bill Downie and are the numerical equivalents of the name of Jesus. In this case, there are three of them set out as musical intervals, and the mediums have used them with great success while conducting séances.

Postscript

The most recent experiments on consciousness conducted by Dr Peter Fenwick, a neuro-psychiatrist at London University, suggest that the visions of people who have experienced a near death experience (NDE) after having a heart attack are valid. The doctor concludes that the *'Study and other evidence points to the mind and the brain not being identical and it appears that the mind may operate in part outside the brain as a sort of field which works the same way as a TV receiver receives programmes through the airwaves'*. This description precisely fits the parameters to qualify variously as the 'Zero Point Field', 'The Akashic Records', 'Morphogenetic Fields' and the 'Collective Unconscious'.

It is fast becoming impossible to ignore the mounting scientific evidence not only that consciousness exists outside the brain and is indeed more than the sum of its parts, but that consciousness interacts with the external world in a very real manner. It is sobering to realise that mystics and sorcerers have said the same thing for millennia and yet successive religions denied and attempted to suppress this fundamental knowledge for their own ends. The time is coming when those who attempt to deny the truth must ultimately accept defeat and admit they are wrong. As Aldous Huxley once said, *'The brain does not create the mind, it inhibits it'*.

END

Sources and References

Exorcism, Understanding Exorcism in Scripture and Practice: by Fr. Jeremy Davis, pub Catholic Truth Society, ISBN 978-1860825026.
American Exorcism, Expelling Demons in the Land of Plenty: by Michael M Cuneo, pub Bantam Books ISBN: 13: 978-0385501767
Hostage to the Devil: The Possession and Exorcism of Five Americans: by Malachi Martin, pub Harper Collins ISBN: 13: 978-0060653378
The Physical Phenomena of Mysticism: by Fr. Herbert Thurston SJ, republished 2007 by Roman Catholic Books ISBN 1-978-929291-91-5
The Omega Project: by Kenneth Ring pub Morrow ISBN 9780688107291
Secret Places, Hidden Sanctuaries: by Klimsezuk and Warner, pub Sterling ISBN 978-1-4027-6207-9
Satan: a Biography: by P.G. Maxwell-Stewart, pub Amberley ISBN 978-1-4456-05750-3
Demons! The Devil Possession & Exorcism: by Anthony Finlay pub Blandford ISBN 0-7137-2720-9
Poltergeists: A History of Violent Ghostly Phenomena: by P.G Maxwell-Stuart pub Amberley, ISBN 978-1-84868-987-9
The Satanic Bible: By Anton Szandor LaVey pub Avon Books ISBN 0-380-01539-0

Websites visited

en.wikipedia.org/wiki/Nicole_Aubrey
en.wikipedia.org/wiki/Urbain_Grandier
en.wikipedia.org/wiki/Loudun_possessions
en.wikipedia.org/wiki/Exorcism
en.wikipedia.org/wiki/Cabin_fever
en.wikipedia.org/wiki/Christian_worship
en.wikipedia.org/wiki/Evangelicalism
en.wikipedia.org/wiki/Matthew_Ashimolowo -
carlomac.net/angels/Laon.html
www.enspirepress.com/...exorcism/spirit_possession_exorcism.html
www.williamhkennedy.com/witchcraft.html

assets.cambridge.org/052181/3239/excerpt/0521813239_excerpt.pdf

www.levity.com/alchemy/h_fre.html -

www.rickross.com/reference/tv_preachers/tv_preachers4.html

www.apologeticsindex.org/m26ad.html

www.newadvent.org/cathen/13750a.htm -

www.nytimes.com/1988/01/10/books/astrtal-bodies-and-tantric sex.

www.equip.org/PDF/JAW755-1.pdf

www.guardian.co.uk/world/2009/apr/11/kingsway-international-chr...

www.forbes.com/sites/mfonobongnsehe/2011/06/07/the-five-richest-pastors-in-...

www.gospelassemblyfree.com/facts/falseprophets.htm

www.sarahefron.com/stories/arctichysteria.shtml

http://www.tldm.org/news/martin.htm

angelqueen.org/articles/07_02_martin_wilson.shtml

www.thebereancall.org/content/popes-failed-exorcism

www.newadvent.org/cathen/07457a.htm

www.kathrynkuhlman.com

en.wikipedia.org/wiki/Christopher_Neil-Smith

en.wikipedia.org/wiki/Kundalini -

womenshistory.about.com/od/protestant/a/aimee_mcpherson.htm

en.wikipedia.org/wiki/Pope_Honorius_III -

en.wikipedia.org/wiki/Maria_Theresa_Chiramel -

www.vatican.va/...lit_doc_20000409_beat-Mankidiyan_en.html

www.spiritreleasement.org/blog/?p=

www.quantumjumping.com/

www.finerminds.com/mind-power/burt-goldman-quantum-jumping/

11th Dimension Publishing

More books from 11th Dimension Publishing!

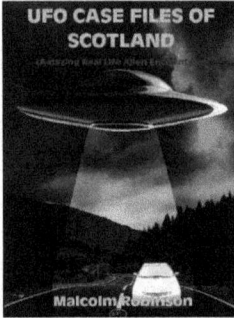

UFO CASE FILES OF SCOTLAND
Malcolm Robinson
978-1-907126-02-4
£14.99

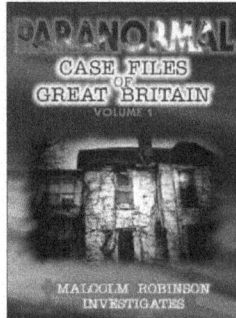

PARANORMAL CASE FILES OF GREAT BRITAIN
VOLUME 1
MALCOLM ROBINSON INVESTIGATES
978-1-907126-06-2
£14.99

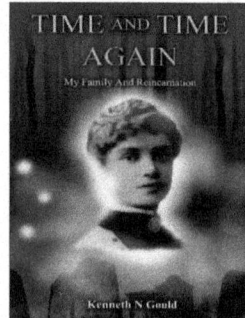

TIME AND TIME AGAIN
My Family And Reincarnation
Kenneth N Gould
978-1-907126-00-0
£9.99

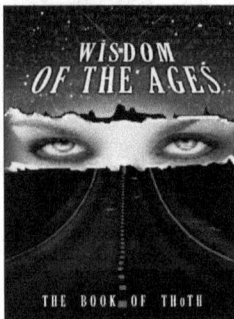

WISDOM OF THE AGES
THE BOOK OF THOTH
978-1-907126-13-0
£10.99

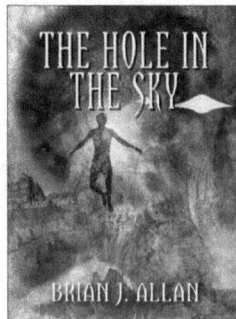

THE HOLE IN THE SKY
BRIAN J. ALLAN
978-1-907126-11-6
£10.99

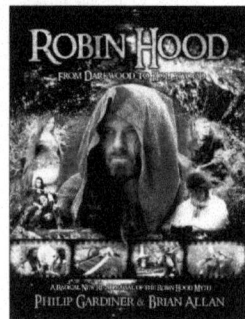

ROBIN HOOD FROM DARKWOOD
PHILIP GARDINER & BRIAN ALLAN
978-1-907126-04-8
£10.99

REVENANTS
HAUNTED PEOPLE & HAUNTED PLACES
BRIAN ALLAN
978-1-907126-05-5
£10.99

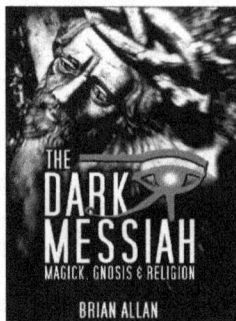

THE DARK MESSIAH
MAGICK, GNOSIS & RELIGION
BRIAN ALLAN
978-1-907126009-3
£10.99

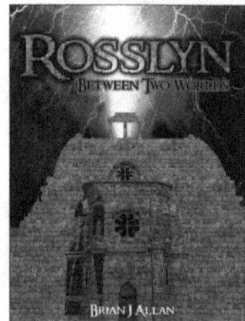

ROSSLYN BETWEEN TWO WORLDS
BRIAN J ALLAN
978-1-907126-10-9
£10.99

www.HealingsOfAtlantis.com

www.ingramcontent.com/pod-product-compliance
Lightning Source LLC
Chambersburg PA
CBHW072135270326
41931CB00010B/1766